THE EVOLUTION OF THE
JILLY JUICE
PROTOCOL

CAN HUMANS LIVE INDEFINITELY
DESPITE THEIR ENVIRONMENT?

JILLIAN MAI THI EPPERLY

Copyright © 2020 Jillian Mai Thi Epperly.

All rights reserved. No part of this book may be reproduced, stored, or transmitted by any means—whether auditory, graphic, mechanical, or electronic—without written permission of the author, except in the case of brief excerpts used in critical articles and reviews. Unauthorized reproduction of any part of this work is illegal and is punishable by law.

The information, ideas, and suggestions in this book are not intended as a substitute for professional medical advice. Before following any suggestions contained in this book, you should consult your personal physician. Neither the author nor the publisher shall be liable or responsible for any loss or damage allegedly arising as a consequence of your use or application of any information or suggestions in this book.

ISBN: 978-1-71694-359-1 (sc)

Because of the dynamic nature of the Internet, any web addresses or links contained in this book may have changed since publication and may no longer be valid. The views expressed in this work are solely those of the author and do not necessarily reflect the views of the publisher, and the publisher hereby disclaims any responsibility for them.

Any people depicted in stock imagery provided by Getty Images are models, and such images are being used for illustrative purposes only.
Certain stock imagery © Getty Images.

Lulu Publishing Services rev. date: 05/29/2020

Necessary Legal Disclaimer:

**The Protocol Recipe has not been evaluated by the Food and Drug Administration. The Protocol is not intended to diagnose, treat, cure or prevent any disease. Consult your physician before beginning any program. The testimonials, statements and opinions presented are applicable to the individuals depicted and are not paid, nor were the contributors provided with any free products, services or other benefits in exchange. The testimonials are representative of protocol user experience but exact results and experience will be unique and individual.

Access to the Jilly Juice LLC Facebook Group:

A percentage of your payment for this book will give you free access to the private Facebook Support Group. Please email jillyjuice1974@gmail.com with a clear photograph of your receipt so we can cross reference the numbers and add you to the group. Please allow 2-5 days of processing time once you submit proof of purchase.

CONTENTS

Preface ix
Acknowledgements... xi

Chapter 1   Balancing Energy of Body Mind and Spirit 1
Chapter 2   What Is Balancing Life?... 3
Chapter 3   Aging, Reproduction and Death................................17
Chapter 4   Geopolitics, Jilly Juice, and Indefinite Life................ 31
Chapter 5   The Jilly Juice Recipe.. 38
Chapter 6   What to Expect with Jilly Juice and How to Implement . 49
Chapter 7   To (Die)t or Not to (Die)t 62
Chapter 8   Jilly Juice, Unintended Benefits, Plants and Animals 68
Chapter 9   The Kind of People Who Do the Jilly Juice 70

Conclusion Jilly Juice Trifecta of Upgrading 73
Bibliography.. 75

PREFACE

This book is about the new idea of introducing potential indefinite life with the use of homemade fermented cabbage, kale and water mixed with White Table Salt, also known as Jilly Juice. Introducing the idea of indefinite life is not new, but the methodology behind my ideas is very new.

White Table Salt has been demonized in the Medical and Holistic community for a reason. Humans have been dealing with major and minor predispositions for centuries. White Table Salt is a powerful energizing mineral, most people do not want to experience, when dealing with symptoms of cancer, disease, and chronic illness. What if the White Table Salt, paired with the proper chemistry, was used in a way to accelerate real true upgrading to the point of indefinite life, once the predispositions of the humans were understood and addressed? What if pairing the White Table Salt with cabbage, kale, and water fermented down to a predigested state for easier absorption, was the answer? What if pain could work for you, not against you?

Not only will I be introducing the concepts to indefinite life, but also introduce what makes up biodiversity, and your personal microbiome. I will be proposing how viruses, bacteria, fungi, protozoa, and parasites, all began as a protein made up of acids assisting in the growth and evolution of mankind on a continuous basis. I will be establishing evidence your biochemistry, made up of fatty acids, amino acids, prohormones and minerals need to be balanced properly to prolong your life expectancy.

I will be exemplifying how the Periodic Tables and biodiversity are connected impacting geopolitics, biological constructs and societal constructs. Biodiversity, in general is made up of viruses, bacteria, fungi, protozoa, parasites and proteins. Once mankind understands everything is connected by a single celled organism, creating large populations all over the world, forging different belief systems, we can then change the trajectory of humanity looping. The Jilly Juice is meant to interrupt the repeated looping sequence of life, death and reproduction cycle to a continuous indefinite life of adaptation and energetic productivity. Balancing biodiversity with the proper balance of the constituents of these agents of biodiversity, is the key to the Jilly Juice Protocol.

ACKNOWLEDGEMENTS

A special acknowledgement to my husband, Stanley J. Epperly, my supporter/investor, Kevin Van Rompaey and Laurie LaRock, my friend and supporter, Lilian Zigering, investor/supporter, Brigitte Le, and light Editor, Linda K. Armstrong, for investing your time and energy into this venture. I could not have done this without all of you!! I especially want to thank all my fans who have helped me iron out my concepts and corrected my Science. They asked for nothing in return except to make sure I have the correct information. I am truly grateful and lucky to have all of you on my journey.

CHAPTER 1

Balancing Energy of Body Mind and Spirit

In the beginning of discovering the Jilly Juice Protocol, it was imperative that I understood that everything is energy.

"The first law of thermodynamics, also known as the law of conservation of energy, states that energy can neither be created nor destroyed; energy can only be transferred or changed from one form to another [1]."

If energy can neither be created or destroyed, then I had to learn how to convert "bad" energy into "good" energy. But who determines what is good energy and what is bad energy? This realization sparked my journey of intellectually understanding how the Jilly Juice Protocol of fermented cabbage and kale juice created the life-giving energy, also known as "good" energy, overriding the "bad" energy or the death energy.

Why is the death energy the "bad" energy? I had to prove my belief in balancing the Body, Mind and Spirit all aligned, living physically on this Earth indefinitely, under the right conditions if the Laws of Life were adhered to properly. This would mean that I did not believe people should physically die, leaving their Spirit or hormones, missing their DNA and RNA, to be stuck floating around the Universe, expressing their hormones at the time of their death over and repeatedly. Kind of like a constant loop of a broken record waiting to become a single celled organism, yet again.

"What is the spirit?" you ask. The spirit is the compilation of the hormones that are expressed by the human based upon the balance or imbalance of the body. The mind takes cues from the spirit and the body working in concert, even if they are misaligned. Before I could even offer that as a possibility, I had to balance out and align my own Body, Mind and Spirit with my body first being balanced out correctly.

Next, once I started cleaning out "the cobwebs" out of my body, I noticed my mind started to think clearer than before. Then, with the mind being clearer and more methodical in my approach, I felt more relaxed which gave off more of a calming spirit to my environment. Therefore, the body must be very balanced, clear and free from disparities to get reasonable thought processes and sensible hormonal manifestations. The expressions of the hormones at different times, will cater to a life trajectory or a death trajectory. This is also based upon man-made law, as well as natural law, with natural law trumping man-made law. Man-made laws are laws of the society and community and biological manipulations, through hormone replacement therapy, immunotherapy protocols and surgical procedures.

No matter how many times man-made law intercepts the Body, Mind and Spirit and society, Mother Nature or natural law will supersede, even the most advanced techniques. Why is that? Because, there are two absolutes in the world, which are: life and death. Before understanding how we can potentially live indefinitely, first I had to understand the Laws of Life, and then the Laws of Death, and what components make up life, and how the environment and biodiversity work symbiotically together.

CHAPTER 2

What Is Balancing Life?

The most profound revelation around the Jilly Juice Protocol is, how to balance out your Body, Mind and Spirit within an environment constantly fluctuating. I was taught to avoid poisons, pathogens, toxins and "chemicals" throughout my entire life. Who determines what is poisonous and pathogenic? We have government agencies like the FDA ("Food and Drug Administration") applying principles to determine what is relatively safe to consume for the general population, but individuals must determine what is appropriate for their own Body, Mind and Spirit. Before an individual can accurately determine how to balance out their own Body, Mind and Spirit, they must understand what their environment and life consists of. Then, they can attempt to balance out their own life in a beneficial way.

What is Life?

Life is biodiversity.

"The term ***biodiversity*** (from "biological diversity") refers to the variety of life on Earth at all its levels, from genes to ecosystems, and can encompass the evolutionary, ecological, and cultural processes that sustain life" [2]. Additionally, your personal microbiome is made up of a trillion little bacteria helping you adapt to your environmental ecosystem.

*The **microbiome** is the genetic material of all the microbes - bacteria, fungi, protozoa and viruses - **that live on and inside the human body**. The number of genes in all the microbes in one person's **microbiome** is 200 times the number of genes in the human genome [26].*

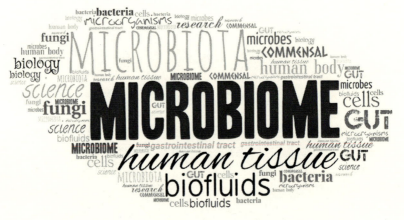

"Microbiome" by Ben Taylor55 is licensed under CC BY 2.0

Viruses, bacteria, fungi, protozoa, parasites and proteins make up all of biodiversity and your microbiome. Mother Nature keeps a balance of all biodiversity according to her intentions. Not only are animals, insects and plants made up of viruses, bacteria, fungi, protozoa, parasites and proteins, but the human microbiome is also made up of them, as well. To go a bit deeper, humans are also made up of fatty acids, amino acids, prohormones and minerals that also must work symbiotically with the environment or elements on the periodic tables and other life forms, also known as biodiversity. Additionally, all of biodiversity send messages through biochemistry to their counterparts based upon the laws applied, or the influences of the internal or external environment. In order for these messages to be accepted relative to the intentions, the environment, which is made up of elements and compounds on the periodic tables, also must be factored in to determine if the Laws of Life or the Laws of Death will be applied. It really comes down to balance, adaptation and energy. All biodiversity has a balance of life within each cell that makes up each organism and the cycle of life loops infinitely, like infinite fractals. All of life can be broken down to energy or protons, neutrons and electrons. These are all under the influence of the external elements in the environment and the internal elements within each cell, and each cell within each organism, and each organism within each ecological location. It is like going from the micro to the macro. There is no one type of life form more important over the other, however, we must understand what makes up biodiversity creating all life forms.

Proteins.

Proteins are single celled organisms that make up cells in bacteria, fungi, protozoa, and parasites and they grow on various carbon sources for synthesis [13]. There are viral proteins NOT made up of cells but made up of a single virus particle known as a *virion,* made up of DNA and RNA genetic material [19]. Carbon sources in cells made up of proteins are various forms of organic and inorganic compounds such as minerals and elements [14]. The Periodic Table of Elements is a perfect example of all the known minerals or elements and compounds and scientists are always discovering new ones. **_Scientists have proven that the first foldable protein was created by at least 10 amino acids in a very salty environment between 3.5 and 3.9 billion years ago [15]._** This type of organism that can live metabolically in a very salty environment, is called a halophile.

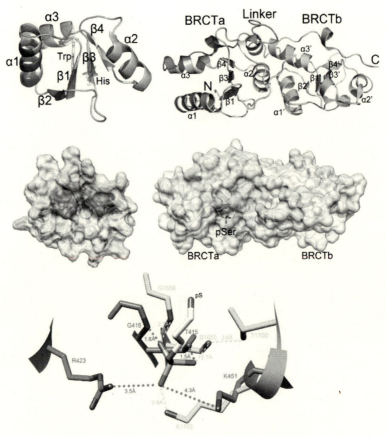

"Figure 3" by <u>Libertas Academica</u> is licensed under <u>CC BY 2.0</u>

The functions of a protein are as follows [18]:

a. *Antibody Proteins:* They bind to foreign particles such as viruses and bacteria to keep the balance within the body. This is also called Immunoglobulin (IgG).
b. *Enzyme Proteins:* They influence the body with cellular chemical reactions, reading new genetic information stored in the DNA by the formation of new molecules.
c. *Messenger Proteins:* These are the types of hormonal proteins that send messages to the body dictating biological processes between the cells, organs and the body's 11 different systems.

a. Circulatory System, Urinary System, Endocrine System, Digestive System, Male/Female Reproductive System, Nervous System, Skeletal System, Respiratory System, Integumentary System, Lymphatic System, and Muscular System.
d. *Structural Component Proteins:* These proteins provide support and structure to the cells. On a larger scale, these proteins allow the body to move.
e. *Transport and Storage Proteins:* These proteins bind and carry atoms within the cells throughout the body.

While proteins are what make up cells and DNA and RNA, the amount of proteins from viruses, fungi, bacteria, protozoa and parasites is what triggers imbalances causing infection triggering antibody proteins to keep the balance. Eventually, antibodies agglutinate, causing reinfection within the body [35].

Viruses.

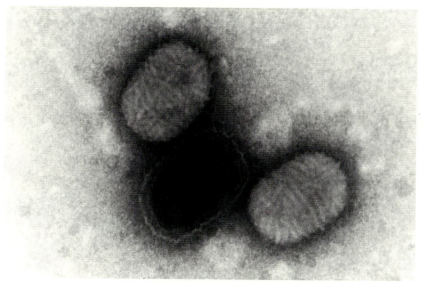

"File:Molluscum contagiousum virus.jpg" by User:Graham Beards is licensed under CC BY-SA 3.0

Viruses are very misunderstood proteins, which act like parasites who determine the life or the death of their host. Viral proteins do not have cell structure. Instead, they consist of a single virus particle known as a virion, which is made of DNA and RNA genetic material [19]. Fundamentally, a virus is an advanced form of data looking to upgrade a body, or replicate so fast, they overwhelm the body, and shut down vital organs. **Viruses are the key to evolution or devolution.**

> *"A virus is made up of a core of genetic material, either DNA or RNA, surrounded by a protective coat called a capsid which is made up of protein. Sometimes the capsid is surrounded by an additional spikey coat called the envelope. [16].*

What determines the actions of the viruses to evolve or devolve the organism? It is energy from the elements, compounds and genetic information influencing the internal and external environment of the host. This will determine how the organism is able to balance out its own biochemistry and adapt to the fluctuating conditions of both its internal and external environment.

Viruses are microscopic parasites, or communicable agents generally much smaller than bacteria. They lack the capacity to thrive and reproduce outside of a host body. Predominantly, viruses have a reputation for being the cause of contagion [3] or evolution. The evolution of man has to do with man's ability to adapt to his environment and he does not do it alone. He is surrounded by viruses, bacteria, fungi, protozoa, parasites and proteins and they all have a role.

> *Viral evolution refers to the heritable genetic changes that a virus accumulates during its lifetime, which can arise from adaptations in response to environmental changes or the immune response of the host. Because of their short generation times and large population sizes, viruses can evolve rapidly [20].*

Since viruses are made up of core DNA or RNA, some viruses are more communicable over others. This happens when:

> *Some RNA viruses embed transcriptase enzymes that transfer RNA virus to DNA virus and combine into the host DNA. Then it follows the DNA replication process. Replication*

usually happens in the cytoplasm. DNA viruses are mostly double-stranded while RNA viruses are single-stranded [17]

When viruses start replicating due to favorable conditions of their host, it happens on an infinite basis, and everything in their environment gets exposed to the new viral information. When amino acids create proteins, and virus proteins hold genetic material and synthesize with a host protein, the genetic material upload from the viruses control cells and their ability to replicate based upon adaptation. This is like a free software upload you get on the World Wide Web. Some people can benefit greatly from the free upload, others will find it very difficult to take on that upload due to their own inability to adapt to new information or their device has limited memory. All cells in biodiversity, are made up of proteins and acids. Acids are made up of carbon, oxygen, hydrogen, and sulfur which are all on the Periodic Tables of Elements. Additionally, these elements are made up of protons, neutrons and electrons and can thrive on combustible energy from the Sun's proton to proton chain or be completely inert, inhibiting energy [22].

"File:Periodic Table Name Symbol Atomic Number and Mass. jpg" by Christinelmiller is licensed under CC BY-SA 4.0

Fungi.

"Fungi" by oatsy40 is licensed under CC BY 2.0

When first discovering the Jilly Juice Protocol, I was under the impression that Candida, which is an overabundance of yeast fungus, was the root cause of all cancer, disease and chronic illness and autoimmunity. This was incorrect. Imbalances in the yeast along with other chemical imbalances in the body, are the root cause of death and disease in humanity. Fungus is a good guy, but when its host is imbalanced, fungus can be perceived as the bad guy.

> *Like bacteria, fungi play an essential role in ecosystems because they are decomposers and participate in the cycling of nutrients by breaking down organic and inorganic materials to simple molecules. Fungi often interact with other organisms, forming beneficial or mutualistic associations [23].*

Fungus plays a vital role in expediting and simplifying the body's ability to adapt to its environment. Like anything, when the fungus is overabundant due to microbiome imbalances, such as the host eating too much of a "good" thing, without the proper balance of chemistry, the excess nutrients and minerals that feed the fungus trigger the fungus to multiply at a faster rate. Therefore, people experience fungal infections. Antibodies, which are the body's defensive proteins, develop from the excess, to keep the balance. Like any life form, fungi evolution is dependent on the state of its environment and the ability to process the environment. This is where viruses play a very important role in the evolution or the devolution of biodiversity, and how they play an important role in fungal evolution. This is most likely predicated upon the intention of the host, but nonetheless, fungi and viruses can work symbiotically together with a common goal, advancing each other as well as the host. It is again, a chain reaction of events which happen infinitely.

Mycoviruses.

Mycoviruses are viruses that infect fungi by inserting their data upload from their single stranded RNA [4]. In turn, the mycovirus has now made itself part of the internal eco-system of the organism. How the organism adapts to the new message upload from the virus, will be relative to the predispositions of the organism being affected. Moreover, the organism's ability or inability to adapt to the current environment properly will also be a determining factor in how the virus affects its host. If the organism is maladaptive to its environment, the messages from the mycovirus is to devolve the organism by rapidly replicating the cells it inhabited. Therefore, vital organs start shutting down due to the body being overwhelmed to the point of imbalance. On the other hand, if the organism is strong enough to handle the message from the mycovirus, the organism will evolve and become more advanced relative to its abilities and Mother Nature's intentions. This is how biodiversity becomes stronger and more evolved. The ability to adapt is the determining factor of survival of the fittest, coined by Charles Darwin, a well-known English naturalist, best known for his contribution to the Science of Evolution [5].

Bacteria.

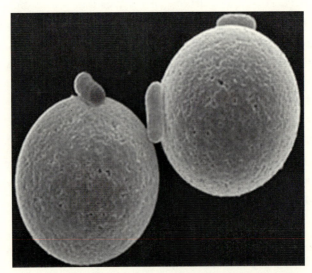

*"Immunomagnetic Bead Selection of E. coli"
by NIAID is licensed under CC BY 2.0*

Throughout the research process, I have made several distinctions about what is "good bacteria" or what is "bad bacteria" based upon the perceptions of the Medical/Holistic industry, and I need to clarify. There are no good or bad bacteria, it is just the different types of bacteria and what they are used for and why.

> *Bacteria play important roles in the global ecosystem. The cycling of nutrients such as carbon, nitrogen, and sulfur is completed by their ceaseless labor. Decomposition is the breakdown of these organisms, and the release of nutrients back into the environment, and is one of the most important roles of the bacteria [24].*

Bacteria play a role in breaking down food and nutrients to a predigested state, to make it easier for the organism to digest and gain benefit from a food source. The very nature of trillions of little bacteria breaking food down, is like having trillions of little stomachs doing the work for you. When people use too many "natural" or "synthetic" antibiotics, which is anti-life or anti-bacterial, they inhibit the ability of the bacteria to break down your food sources for easier absorption, digestion and then evolution.

Some bacteria you only need in small amounts, and some bacteria, you need in larger amounts, but not too much. When certain elements on the periodic table are used with the intention to control certain bacteria, they can control their reproduction but not necessarily kill them. It is impossible to kill all bacteria, but it is possible to control their population growth in a controlled environment and render them temporarily chemically inert [25]. Again, like any life form, it is subject to evolve or devolve based upon the conditions of the internal and external environment of the organism. Viruses evolve bacteria and its host to either upgrade or downgrade the host's ability to evolve. A bacterium with a virus taking up residence in its cells are also called Bacteriophages.

Bacteriophages.

Bacteriophages work the same way. When a new virus enters the environment of its host, it will upload its genetic information into the bacteria, thus uploading valuable data which will send messages to the rest of the organism based upon intention and adaptive or maladaptive traits. Evolution is based upon very strong adaptive qualities and therefore, mankind can adapt to all sorts of temperatures, geographical locations and even predispositions. However, in America, the time between reproduction and death seems to be getting shorter and shorter with more predispositions to endure throughout a person's lifetime until death [7]

Parasites.

In my last book, published in 2018, which has been since discontinued, I characterized parasites as something to fear, kill and get rid of. I was under the impression that parasites were foreign objects that needed to be purged, at all costs. This was incorrect. Like any form of biodiversity on this Earth, parasites have a place and role.

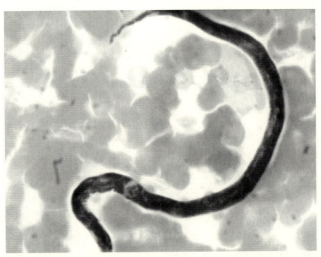

"Microfilaria of loa loa x100mag (1)UK NEQAS" by *Biology Open Educational Resources* is licensed under *CC BY-SA 2.0*

There are three main classes of parasites that keep the balance in biodiversity. They are protozoa, helminths, and ectoparasites. Some can cause disease in humans, and others have no effect other than help the host mineralize nutrients for easier absorption [28]. One example of a beneficial protozoa parasite is pinworms, which are usually found in children. They live around the rectum and they consume bacteria and other waste material from the human. Their role is not pathogenic and usually, pinworms go away as the child matures and is able to process and clean their own internal ecosystem [29].

Some ectoparasites such as fleas and ticks can be pathogenic due to the imbalances of lactic acid within the organism's body. Rapid reproduction of parasitized blood seems to thrive better in an environment rich with lactic acid build up according to scientific experiments [30]. Additionally, mosquitoes, are another example of an ectoparasite as a virus vector causing disease in a human. Not all mosquitoes are infectious passing along communicable diseases, however, if the mosquito is infected, they will infect the host they feed upon [84].

Helminths are intestinal parasites that serve a function to keep the microbiome balanced enough for the host to carry out their day to day activities. They exist because they are attracted to the breath and other secretions of the host who is sending off chemical signals, that it needs help metabolizing its environment. Therefore, there are very distinctive odors coming from organisms who have lactic acid imbalances [31]. Helminths serve as an intermediary between the microbiome and the host's ability to process chemical messages. If the microbiome is off balance, the chemical message becomes convoluted, hence the helminth responds to the chemistry of the host, as if they were invited by the chemical messages.

> *Although competition between helminths for food resources, secretion of bacterial growth inhibitors by some species, and host age and diet have all been proposed as mechanisms altering the gut microbiota, the interplay between host, helminths and microbiota has attracted much attention owing to the potential for helminths to induce direct or indirect changes in the microbiota [31]*

Protozoa.

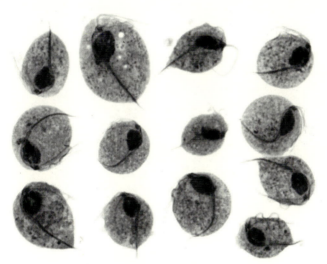

"File:Trichomonas (01).jpg" by isis325
is licensed under CC BY 2.0

Like any single celled, or multi-celled plantlike or fungus like organism living in groups, protozoa have a role in keeping the balance in biodiversity. Strictly consumers, living off carbohydrate and bacteria as its sole source of energy, protozoa keep the balance by consuming plant or animal matter, which gives it energy, thus energizing the host it is feeding from. Their role is to mineralize nutrients making it more bioavailable for the environment, releasing nitrogen into the environment [27]. Protozoa parasites are also intermediaries between the host and the microbiota balancing out the microbiome as needed. The chemical messages secreted though pores and breath are like invitations to the protozoa parasites to come in and take up residence.

Viruses can take up residence in a parasite that has taken up residence in your microbiome, much like an infinite fractal that is made of concentric objects that share the same center axis and go to infinity. This is commonly known as viral symbiont of a protozoan parasite. It has been suggested that the genetic data in the parasite and the inserted data from the virus are especially more pathogenic to the human. If the imbalances of the host call for the need of a parasite intermediary, to help in breaking waste down for easier absorption, then a virus taking up residence in the parasite could be significantly more deadly relative to how imbalanced the human is. The inflammatory response of antibodies rapidly accumulating from the body-triggered viral symbiont can be especially rapid causing major discomfort to the host. The common practice of human hosts experiencing this, is to turn to antibiotics, also known as anti-life, to control the cells holding the aggressive data upload from the virus controlling the parasite affecting the human [32]. Instead of using beneficial bacteria coupled with the proper chemistry and, nutritive elements to control the entities in the Microbiome [83], the health and wellness industries apply aggressive "chemicals" to stagnate bacterial, viral protein and fungi replication. The practices of inhibiting cell replication, inducing antibodies with Cannabis Oil, Chemotherapy and other aggressive immunotherapies and Holistic remedies, in reaction to anomalies, cause people to age, reproduce and then die. You are your Microbiome and you are your environment. If you practice killing things in your body, you are slowly killing yourself, which is the aging process. I will go more in depth, in the next chapter.

CHAPTER 3

Aging, Reproduction and Death

Aging is Malabsorption.

If the First Law of Thermodynamics is about energy being neither created nor destroyed, then, The Second Law of Thermodynamics is about the *quality* of energy. It states that as energy is transferred or transformed, more and more of it is wasted [6].

In the beginning of my discovery of the protocol, I blamed the overfed yeast, called Candida, as the sole culprit for why people had malabsorption issues. Well, as soon as I delved deeper into the science of what makes up the human body, I discovered imbalances in the fatty acids, amino acids, prohormones and minerals, triggering antibodies to over accumulate, and cause Malabsorption Syndrome [8].

When the rate of energy, nutrients, minerals, enzymes, bacteria, nutrients and acids leave the body faster than its ability to absorb and work correctly, it becomes wasted energy, and then anomalous functions of the body start getting triggered. This is when diagnosis of cancer, disease, chronic illness and autoimmunity happen, because of the rapid replication of anomalous cells, with no balancing forces. Without going heavily into the detailed rabbit holes of virus behavior in the genomes, the human's ability to adapt to the virus taking up residence in their bacteria and yeast (yeast also being a type of fungus normal to the body), is predicated upon how weak or strong the human body is. How many people have been exposed to the influenza virus or been coughed on by a sick person, but never trigger any symptoms? How many people have received vaccines (attenuated virus) and never had an adverse reaction? Many people have been exposed to influenza and received vaccines and are asymptomatic. You can argue they have an overactive immune system, which could be a valid argument, or maybe their immune system and body was very strong at the time of exposure.

What would then cause the body to systematically degrade, or age after the point of maturity, or even before the point of maturity? The answer would be, humans born with predispositions triggered by trauma and maladaptive traits, which were never addressed and reversed with the right chemistry, compounding each generation.

Additionally, the immune system activates by the need to keep the vital organs functioning and is a type of **_biochemical triage_**, the ability of the body to determine a priority of need when finding resources to keep the body alive. For example, when the reserves of minerals and nutrients are low due to malabsorption, the body will steal resources from the hair, skin, nails, and bones to send to the vital organs. This shows up as balding, graying hair, papery thin skin and osteoporosis diagnosis. Minerals are being depleted from the body due to malabsorption. This malabsorption, or the Second Law of Thermodynamics, creates the perfect environment for the diagnosis of cancer, disease, chronic illness and autoimmunity. When a person is diagnosed with cancer, disease, chronic illness, and autoimmunity, it is the body's way of sending signals to the brain that there is something wrong, please do something different and fix the issue. However, the human does not know what to do, so they do not give the body what it needs and the issues are masked, or the cells die, transferring that energy onto other organs and cells in the body causing chain reactions of disease. These maladaptive traits, which are traits exhibiting the inability to function at the optimal level, get compounded every generation.

Moreover, these maladaptive traits triggered from the imbalances in the internal and external environment encourage more discrepancies in the bacteria, fatty acids, amino acids, prohormones and minerals. These nutrients, proteins, and acids make up the building blocks of the cells, while the bacteria, fungus (yeast) and viruses act as messengers dictating the functions of the body. When the body notices antigen entering the body, chemical defenders get produced, also known as lymphocytes and proteins producing antibodies [88]. Antigen is any excess bacteria, fatty acid, amino acid, prohormone, mineral and virus entering and remaining in the body causing imbalances. Additionally, if it's a new organism entering the environment, the body produces antibodies to seek and control and keep the balance as well as keep the foreign organisms at bay. Imbalances in biochemistry cause entropy or decline in thermal energy. When the body fails to release the excess antibodies, they accumulate causing more cellular imbalances in the lymph nodes and other systems. They may also come up as benign or malignant tumors or cancer clusters, because of abnormal cellular replication. Those antibodies work against the 11 different systems; therefore, people contract cancer and disease and potentially death. Malabsorption is the body's inability to process the nutrients and minerals correctly and regenerate cells at an exponential level.

Anti-Biotic is Anti-Life.

When you inhibit life on the micro level, you inhibit life at the macro level triggering reproduction and then death. I will cover reproduction associated with this concept later. Weaknesses addressed incorrectly, trigger cancer, disease and chronic illnesses. The methodologies used in the Allopathic/Holistic world create more weaknesses and imbalances that viruses, bacteria, fungi, protozoa, parasites, proteins and excess minerals take advantage of. The Allopathic/Holistic industry loves to try to control all life forms at the micro level, influencing the macro level, using different elements, minerals, acids and hormones. However, the practice of inhibiting cellular regeneration does not come without its consequences. Natural or deemed "synthetic" antibiotic, antimicrobial, antiparasitic, anti-inflammatory, antifungal, and antibacterial is anti-life, **inhibiting cell replication**. It throws your microbiome off balance by inhibiting cells and life to replicate. Therefore, this practice stops the deep cellular regeneration at the micro level to the macro level. Eventually, vital organs shut down. However, before vital organs start shutting down, some people trigger reproduction and become pregnant, before the micro level destruction influences the death process at the macro level. So, while applying these methodologies, some of these protocols not only inhibit cell replication, at the micro level, they also feed the fungus and bacteria and parasites causing infections. Then, applying anti-inflammatories to manage infection, keeps up with the vicious cycle of anti-biotic lifestyles, until the person subsequently become very fertile, or completely shuts down their own vital organs.

Honey, pills, powders, supplements, detoxes, heavy minerals, colloidal silver, garlic, all types of spices used with the intention of anti-biotic or anti-inflammatory for pain, heavy metal detoxes, turmeric, Cipro, CBD oil, essential oils, cannabis, kombucha, elderberry syrup, and apple cider vinegar are some examples of prescription, over the counter or natural anti-biotics [87]. So, when you are taking a natural or synthetic antibiotic, you are inhibiting cell replication of all forms of life in your body which is you. Immune suppression through surgical procedures, ALL types of therapies, drugs, and the abovementioned anti-biotics/anti-inflammatories, are one of the biggest mistakes of the Holistic/Allopathic industry when it comes to triggering indefinite life. It is like taking two steps forward, temporarily, but taking ten steps back. These practices threaten individual human longevity. When the Second Law of Thermodynamics is being applied from the body, misusing the energy it takes in, combined with bodies stagnated in their filtration or elimination processes, the results are, people who have imbalances in their fatty acids, amino acids, prohormones and minerals. Inhibiting life replication at the micro level, will cause you to be very fertile at the macro level, which I will explain later. This behavior will trigger the body to reproduce, because it is sensing you are inhibiting life, and it must reproduce, or else trigger extinction of your genetic line.

Currently Humanity Is Stuck in a Loop.

Just think of the four seasons, Winter, Spring, Summer and Fall.

1. Winter is like the death process, a stagnancy in life, or an upset of homeostasis. Animals hibernate, some trees lose their leaves and fruit bearing trees are taking a temporary nap waiting for warm sunshine.
2. Spring is a rebirth of plants, insects and animals, as trees drop their seeds and new flowers and bushes start growing and developing.

Little birds are incubating in their eggs and bunnies are having litters and litters of baby bunnies all enjoying the beautiful spring air and warm sunshine.

3. Summer is like a period of growth and sustaining maturity for organisms with shorter lifespans, and it is a period of life and stability for organisms with longer life spans like mammals and reptiles.
4. Fall is the period of slow degradation getting prepared for the winter hibernation (death). It is when the urgency to store food and fat is paramount, for animals and humans to hunker down for the long cold Winter.

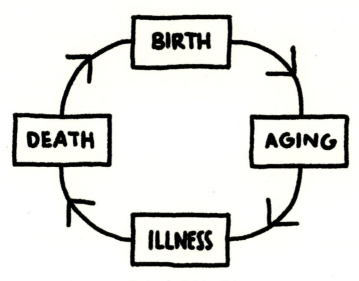

Design by Brigitte Le

Currently, the human body works the same way too. We have birth, maturity, degradation and death looping over and repeatedly every generation, with each generation reinventing the wheel. Like, repackaging the same ideas repetitively. Below is the current human cycle of birth, adaptation and death we need to interrupt:

1. *Adaptation/Rebirth*
2. *Pain/Upgrading/Mucus/Poop*
3. *Disease/Mucus Suppression/Antibody Accumulation/Therapy/PTSD*

4. *Indefinite Death is the Final Energy Transfer of a Multi-Cellular Life Form*
   The Cycle Starts Again
5. *Adaptation/Rebirth*
6. *Pain/Upgrading/Mucus/Poop*
7. *Disease/Mucus Suppression/Antibody Accumulation/Therapy/PTSD*
8. *Indefinite Death is the Final Energy Transfer of a Multi-Cellular Life Form*

Adaptation/Rebirth.

Adaptation in humans mitigates human extinction. It is either a birth of a new baby, or a human making voluntary or involuntary biochemical changes, based upon the internal and external environment. All the different therapies, foods, environmental regulations and medicines, assist all humans to adapt to their environment on a deeper level or superficial level. Some adapt better than others. However, when you apply the wrong chemistry to the biochemistry over time relative to predispositions, adaptation ceases to become easy and then the body tries to adjust but cannot.

> *"Adaptation…modification of an organism or its parts that makes it more fit for existence under the conditions of its environment: a heritable physical or behavioral trait that serves a specific function and improves an organism's <u>fitness</u> or survival [37].*

Pain/Upgrading/Mucus/Poop.

When the body is continuously trying to adjust and readjust to the weaknesses the body is sustaining, environmental changes, pain and upgrading get triggered. Pain is the genesis of your body upgrading and adapting. Pain, mucus, feces and urine are the body's way of trying to upgrade and adjust to the new environment. However, constant anomalous pain, constant mucus, constant anomalous feces, and urination anomalies, are the body's way of trying to upgrade and you are not giving the body what it needs to repair itself. So, with that said, pain is an indicator of imminent life, or imminent death. Normally the body will only release mucus, feces and urine at certain times of the day, like when you wake up or when you are about to go to sleep relative to your food and water intake. But, if you find the release is excessive relative to your habits, you might have an adaptation issue.

Trauma/Disease/Antibody Accumulation/Mucus Suppression/Therapies.

Pain comes from the prostaglandin hormone which aids in the start of the healing process.

> *When tissue is damaged... cause pain, fever and inflammation, which sparks the healing process. Prostaglandins also stimulate the formation of a blood clot and the contraction of the blood vessel wall when your body is bleeding [38].*

The Hippocratic oath sworn by all Doctors in the American Medical Association is the promise to do no harm to their patients. There is a fine line between allowing their patients to writhe in agony or give them something for the pain. All medications have a place and appropriate time. Immune suppression to mitigate pain and symptoms at the request of the patient in therapy is one of the main factors of why humans have never considered indefinite life. When a patient has imbalances in their fatty acids, amino acids, prohormones and minerals and they actively suppress hormones triggered by trauma and cancer, with prostaglandin inhibitors, the Second Law of Thermodynamics is applied [39]. Cold medications, all pills, all types of therapies, powders, supplements, herbs, detoxes, lemon diets, superficial diets, all contribute to immune suppression and, lay the groundwork to trigger reproduction, transferring a new life, or trigger the final energy transfer back into the ground, called death.

Indefinite Death is the Final Energy Transfer of a Multi-Cellular Life Form.

Death is the final energy transfer once the body cannot function without the vital organs. But what if it could be Summer, all year round for humans? What if we did not have to die, or feel the need to reproduce?

We could have a stable environment with no war, indefinite life, no cancer, disease, chronic illness, abuse or crimes.

The process of indefinite death, or energy transference, taken from one entity onto another, becomes a rapid death process. This happens when there is an overabundance of antibodies, triggered by weaknesses in the cells and imbalances in your microbiome, and your biochemistry made up of fatty acids, amino acids, prohormones and minerals. This can happen at the cellular level, the organ level, or at system level, such as the Cardiovascular System.

The leading causes of death are heart attacks, strokes, and acute respiratory disease from imbalances in the microbiome and malnutrition. When oxygen is being blocked from the heart, brain and lungs, from rapid accumulation of antibodies triggered by antigen, you will see people die rapidly or slowly. Death occurs when the rate of antibody accumulation is far greater than the release and the body is malnourished. The Medical/Holistic industry tries to slow down the rapid antibody accumulation by fluids in IV bags made up of saline, glucose and minerals as well as superficial diet changes. Such procedures are not enough when the body is triggering the Second Law of Thermodynamics, which is energy wasted from malabsorption. Further complications arise when over the counter drugs and herbs suppress and dry up the mucus [11]. This causes the body to hold onto the antibodies that eventually do accumulate and shut down the body as well. However, we cannot discount the need for some manmade intermediaries such as man-made law to work in conjunction with natural law. Vaccines and temporary solutions in the Holistic/Allopathic world are a type of therapy. They are meant to work temporarily, but never should be relied on indefinitely, unless you wish to be taken down to a single celled protein before conception.

I have made some assertions that continually reproducing offspring from bodies with major predispositions weakens the overall population. In my research, each generation is getting weaker and weaker with more childhood diseases and cancers. It becomes startling when autism rates rise by 43% in New Jersey [34]. This evidence suggests that reproduction from bodies with major and minor predispositions, have something to do with the rise in autism rates. Additionally, my research also suggests that fertility is a sign of imbalance, when parasite infections aid in the fertility of humans, confirming my suspicions, fertile women may not have a well-balanced biochemistry.

> "... Up to a third of the world's population also lives with such infections.
> But while Ascaris lumbricoides increased fertility in the nine-year study, hookworms had the opposite effect, leading to three fewer children across a lifetime. [33].

Moreover, from my observations of people on social media and in my community, genetic lines are disappearing because of sterility, predispositions, choosing career over family and poverty. Therefore, there is no desire to reproduce, or some women are just not maternally motivated, and that means Americans are not actively making babies to replace themselves [12]. This is all due in part to politics and belief systems, causing antibody accumulation, and the body's inability to release excess antibodies from the body, thus causing anomalies and more weaknesses to all 11 different body systems. Too many antibodies stored in the body will eventually attack vital organs relative to predispositions. However, despite the number of antibodies the body is holding onto, the body does adapt, in some way. This may be the reason why people live for a certain amount of time with their disabilities and weaknesses until the body finally gives out. The West values life, once given the chance at life. When bodies are in a state of decay, but still relatively viable, humans trigger the process of reproduction, also known as sexuality, expressions of love and procreation. This is what causes the aging process, or the systematic degradation of your Body, Mind and Spirit, and this is where reproduction begins, like a continuous loop. Can the Jilly Juice offer us the potential to live life indefinitely, in Body, Mind and Spirit, on this Earth? Before we can answer that question, we must address our beliefs that inhibiting cellular replication on the micro level (your microbiome), will also inhibit life on the macro level (YOU). However, usually, before a person actually dies from inhibiting cellular replication at the macro-level, the reproductive system is triggered, causing fertility and this is how the body mitigates extinction by gene spreading.

Biochemical Imbalances Triggering Reproduction and Cancer.

If the First Law of Thermodynamics is: *energy can neither be created or destroyed*, then death is just another form of energy transfer from one entity to another. Reproduction and epigenetics are the science of how humans mitigate extinction, induce energy transference, and then exhibit how their genes get expressed, based upon the influences of the internal and external environment of the human. Consequently, we have man-made law to mitigate sexual predators from transferring their unwelcome energy upon others. However, before sexual urges happen, imbalances in their microbiome triggering Cancer and diagnosable diseases must happen first. Therefore, men and women become more sexual during their peak times of reproduction from these chemical messages of imbalances, and it can happen at all ages in our society. In order to create a baby, humans must transfer energy between the sperm and the egg. These strong and weak genes get passed down from generation to generation. Each generation becomes weaker than the next until the genetic line stops altogether. Biotechnology potentially helps immunocompromised people to transition to their environment due to imbalances. Too many imbalances in the microbiome pave the way for Cancer to develop.

Cancer comes from imbalances in your microbiome. When you have imbalances in your microbiome, comprised of viral data, bacteria, protein, fungi, protozoa, and parasites, those imbalances will cause infection. Infection induces antibody production and weakens different parts of your body causing cells to mutate negatively and then misfire.

Cancer

> *Cancer is the uncontrolled growth of abnormal cells in the body. Cancer develops when the body's normal control mechanism stops working. Old cells do not die and instead grow out of control, forming new, abnormal cells. These extra cells may form a mass of tissue, called a tumor. Some cancers, such as leukemia, do not form tumors [92]*

In turn, more antibodies get created to keep the balance. When you have compound weaknesses, antibody accumulation or infection in your microbiome, biochemical imbalances in your fatty acids, amino acids, prohormones and minerals, cause more infections from disturbances in your microbiome. It becomes a never-ending vicious cycle. On top of that, nutritional malabsorption happens along with stagnancy in the digestive processes and lymphatic system. When antibodies accumulate without a proper release of the excess, they will then agglutinate, cause more infection creating benign or malignant tumors from abnormal cells replicating faster over normal healthy cells. Then, the application of antibiotics, antimicrobials, anti-inflammatories, antifungals and antibacterial cause more imbalance because you are feeding and fighting different entities in your body causing more imbalances, and then infection happens. Antibodies get created and the cycle of inhibiting cellular regeneration continues from the micro level, potentially causing fertility and then death at the macro level. When there is not enough life in your body to keep the vital organs going, due to protocols inhibiting the cellular regeneration process, the body shuts down.

Cycle of Imbalances Leading to Cancer Then Death

1. Imbalance in Microbiome (Viruses, Bacteria, Fungi, Protozoa, Parasites, and Proteins) triggering imbalances in your biochemistry made up of fatty acids, amino acids, prohormones and minerals.
2. Infection Occurs at the Microbial Level Triggering Symptoms of Diagnosis like Bacterial Infection, Parasite Infection, Viral Infection, Protozoa (microbial infection), Fungal Infection, Abnormal Protein Cell Functions and Replication, and Benign or Malignant Tumors.
3. Then people administer: Antibiotics, Anti-Inflammatories, Anti-Fungal, Anti-Microbial, Anti-Parasite, Anti-Viral, Immunotherapies, Surgical Procedures, Hormone Replacement Therapies, Prescription Drugs, Over the Counter Drugs, Illicit Drugs and any other remedies, and procedure on the market, get applied causing the feeding and fighting of all entities in your body, triggering biochemical imbalances.

4. Therefore, Imbalance in Microbiome (Viruses, Bacteria, Fungi, Protozoa, Parasites, and Proteins) triggering imbalances in your biochemistry made up of fatty acids, amino acids, prohormones and minerals, occur.
5. Infection Occurs, again, at the Microbial Level Triggering Symptoms of Diagnosis like Bacterial Infection, Parasite Infection, Viral Infection, Protozoa (microbial infection), Fungal Infection, Abnormal Protein Cell Functions. Abnormal Protein Cell Functions and Replication and Benign or Malignant Tumors.
6. Then people administer: Antibiotics, Anti-Inflammatories, Anti-Fungal, Anti-Microbial, Anti-Parasite, Anti-Viral, Immunotherapies, Surgical Procedures, Hormone Replacement Therapies, Prescription Drugs, Over the Counter Drugs, Illicit Drugs and any other remedies, and procedure on the market, get applied causing the feeding and fighting of all entities in your body, triggering biochemical imbalances.

The methodologies used above dealing with imbalances, should only be used temporarily, but they are not. They are used indefinitely. Therefore, this cycle keeps repeating throughout a person's lifetime until the imbalances in the microbiome become so incorrigible, there is nothing left for the Holistic and Allopathic to do, except enroll you into Hospice, where death is inevitable and imminent. Again, sometimes man-made law is necessary, but only on a temporary basis. Vaccines are a type of immunotherapy that is necessary in certain circumstances. The following section will outline the pros and cons of the vaccine industry.

Vaccines and Viruses Can Save You or Degrade You.

Vaccines are a necessary intermediary for anyone not strong enough to take on the environment alone with their current immune system. The elderly, children and the sick need the help of modern medicine, to adapt to their environment. Biotechnology has perfected a way to circumvent the rapid antibody accumulation on a weak body, with a less severe version of the viruses and pathogens in the environment through the vaccine campaigns. This is in the effort to slowly transition the body into the new environment without shocking the system into a rapid death process. However, there have been outcries from activist groups, who do not understand they will experience symptoms when introducing new viruses and bacteria to a body, that will be exposed to the viruses and bacteria, no matter what. Their argument is their children are becoming vaccine injured by the injections. Children and adults, with many aggressive predispositions, will have trouble adjusting to any new environment from the vaccines or their current environmental exposures. This is also why you can have two people receive the same vaccine and both will have different reactions or no reaction from the vaccine at all. No different than when a very healthy person exposed to a sick person never gets sick, while another person must call in sick because of virus exposure. Additionally, the adjuvants that are also in the vaccines are just forms of biochemistry, biodiversity and elements triggering an effective immune response, therefore not dangerous. If we can recall history when the Spanish discovered the Americas, spreading smallpox and taking down American Indian Nations, we can relate to why the CDC ("Centers for Disease Control") require or suggest children and immunocompromised adults get the latest vaccine due to strains of viruses mutating every season [9]. When Third World Countries with high infant mortality rates are visited by the Peace Corps or Doctors without Borders, they start seeing the decline in infant mortality rates. Children, who would have died in the aggressive environment such as in the Sub-Saharan Desert in Africa, were saved by the vaccines. However, their weaknesses were affected and some adverse reactions such as disease, death or disability were the unintended consequence from the vaccine or virus exposure. But this is better than outright dying from an aggressive virus in the environment, going back to a single celled organism, when they have already graduated to conception, and then to an advanced form of a multicellular organism!

Children in America who have major predispositions also experience unintended consequences from virus/antibody exposure in their environment, either in the womb or around a communicable person. There is no way to predetermine how each person is going to adjust to their environment. If one decides to get a titer test to see what antibodies come up triggering a positive, it might give people a clue what the catalyst was triggering a heart attack, stroke, aneurysm, pneumonia or death. Titer tests have conditions set to determine how many antibodies need to be present for protection from antigen or new viruses in the environment [36]. Drug tests work the same way. They test the antibodies to see how recent your exposure was to that illicit drug.

Politicizing life, death and reproduction, is a mainstay in our current political climate, and perceptions of what is life and what is death and who gets to reproduce, will be an ongoing conversation fraught with controversy. However, Jilly Juice could be the answer to most people's questions regarding the meaning of life. Are we meant to die and pass on, or are we meant to continuously live on this Earth physically in Body, Mind and Spirit, indefinitely, barring anything anomalous out of our control?

Politics, religion/spirituality and health all have their own spin on their perceptions of life and death. The Jilly Juice world also has its own perception of life and death. However, life is about law and order, while death is disorder and chaos. In the interest of balancing out the Body, Mind and Spirit, it is optimal society and the human body must abide by Life's Laws of Order as opposed to death's disorder, or entropy and chaos. When life begins from a single celled protein with the help of viruses, bacteria, fungi, protozoa, and parasites, the thought of dying and going back to a single celled organism after reaching the age of a multi-celled mature human being, is not very appealing. Humans are on a constant loop of life and death. Once we understand how to balance the Elements, Biodiversity and Biochemistry, we can then consider the potential for indefinite life.

CHAPTER 4

Geopolitics, Jilly Juice, and Indefinite Life

Indefinite Life

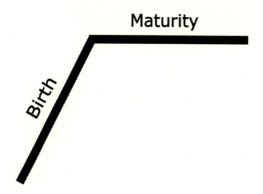

Design by Brigitte Le

Before I understood how to tap into potential indefinite life, I had to understand why the world is split between the haves and the have nots. It came down to the able bodied and the disabled. When the Body, Mind and Spirit are misaligned, disabilities exhibit themselves and the human is not working to their full potential. It does not mean society does not have a place for them, it just means the "disabled" human has limited choices due to their inabilities. Some humans do not have obvious poignant disabilities, thus have far more occupational choices. Their plethora of choices will eventually offer them more opportunities to make a very good living. With such a split, this also translates into legislation, societal constructs merged with biological constructs, and then the fight to balance the budget of a society is implemented according to its needs.

Politicians and lawmakers are very aware of who their constituents are, and they try to meet all their needs, but it does not always translate, and consequently, domestic and international wars happen. The wars between the haves and the have nots happen all the time on a societal level domestically and internationally. Plus, these budget wars trigger the politics and religion and even science beliefs when it comes to the health and wellness industry.

I have been privileged enough to explore all the different fields of politics, religions and science, then making the connections they are all related to each other. It was a matter of slowly and methodically breaking them down to their elemental states. This exercise made me aware of how politics, religion and science are based upon the perceptions of the balance or imbalance of the humans' biochemistry at the time. For example, my perception of God, in religion, was something intangible to me, a few years ago. Now, my perception of the word, God, is a representation of Life, spoken through the eyes of the right brained people. "The right hemisphere is associated with creativity, emotion and intuition" [89]. Conversely, left hemisphere dominance is more logical and organized in approach, hence why left brained people gravitate more to Science and Engineering. Maybe one day we can have everyone use both sides of their brain simultaneously. It could cut out the confusion and misunderstandings between left and right brained humans. My ability to break down the social constructs and biological constructs also fed into my beliefs around life and death and reproduction. In the beginning of my journey of discovering Jilly Juice, I was caught up in some narrow perceptions of life, death and reproduction. My exploration was still very new when I presented my thoughts to the world on the Dr. Phil show. I was still buying into the social constructs dictating biological constructs and we have since discovered, social constructs change all the time based upon the evolution or devolution of society. However, we do not know what a "normal" biological construct is, and we might know one day, once everyone becomes 100% healthy.

Assuming something is normal or not normal is still very premature, in the scheme of things.

In the beginning of the Jilly Juice Protocol rollout, I was facing advertising issues and I was contacted by an agent from the Federal Trade Commission. The agent instructed me to change my advertising on my website or face heavy fines. He said, "There were no absolutes, when it came to cures and remedies." If I wanted to advertise Jilly Juice on a public domain, I had to change my wording. I agreed with him on that point, that Jilly Juice is not a cure, because cures are temporary and not guaranteed. The only absolutes in this world are life and death, or how energy is transferred and converted. As this became clear to me, it became my life goal to differentiate what was life giving and what contributed to the death and reproduction process. I have since discovered it is about balance.

The thought process behind my Jilly Juice Protocol did not start out with the belief that all humans could live indefinitely under the right circumstances. It was from peeling back the layers of "truths" that I was taught ever since childhood, that allowed me to consider the possibility we did not have to die from cancer, disease and chronic illness. What if we could regenerate missing organs, limbs, even if we were born without them? What if all the symptoms in the Allopathic/Holistic world and Jilly Juice, was the body's way to purge out what did not belong, to make room for what did belong, assuming the correct chemistry was applied? What if pain was a sign of upgrading and humans just mischaracterized it causing more pain by applying the wrong chemistry? What if the body held onto fecal matter in our colon and intestines, due to the lack of energetic minerals to wholly release it, contributing to ineffective absorption? What if the waste being held on to in our body was causing DNA methylation, a type of cellular asphyxiation, causing negative mutations to the Body, Mind and Spirit of the human? What if the answer laid within the White Table Salt backed by the proper chemistry?

Salt.

The explanation of the history of Jilly Juice, the mechanisms behind the upgrading symptoms and why White Table Salt is used in the fermentation over pink Himalayan Salt, will address all the rhetorical questions above. When humans have imbalances in their fatty acids, amino acids, prohormones and minerals, they must release the excess, and absorb what is needed. The rate of release of needed nutrients, minerals and acids is far greater in humans exhibiting cancer, disease and chronic illness. Additionally, the rate of over-accumulating antibodies, from antigen (overabundance), in humans, is the sole cause of disease and premature death, covered in *Chapter 3 Aging, Reproduction and Death*. What the body is missing is balance and effectively functioning systems, working in concert together.

When the yeast fungi in the body that serves as a messenger and decomposer becomes overabundant due to over-accumulation of sugar acids, this unbalanced condition causes fungal infections and the body triggers antibody accumulation. Too many antibodies being created from overabundance of antigen not released timely and effectively creates anomalies in cells triggering tumors and followed by cancer cells. The White Table Salt, NaCl, is nature's most powerful mineral source when it comes to energizing minerals, nutrients and acids. I changed the Salt in the protocol from pink Salt, which had too many heavy metals, or "trace minerals" as promoted in the Holistic world, to the iodized or non-iodized White Table Salt. I also do not want people using distilled water. If you get your trace minerals from the air, food and tap water and your environment, there is no need to get more heavy metals from pink Salt in the Jilly Juice. It is redundant and it makes your ferments smellier due to the excess heavy metals.

Heart and Brain.

Your cells have sodium channels that excite and energize your organs and systems to work symbiotically with the available nutrition, acids and minerals [41]. Moreover, you have chloride channels all over your body through your motor neurons as well as receptors in your heart [43], which act as a type of atrial defibrillation when sodium chloride hits those channels. Defibrillators in the medical world are like that extra push. When someone is suffering from a heart attack, first responders use defibrillators to send an electrical impulse to the heart, to jumpstart it again [44]. The potential to survive preexisting conditions such as, heart attacks, strokes and aneurysms is greater when the body is backed by nutrition, lactic acid and water supporting the natural defibrillation, strengthening the weaknesses in the heart, brain and cardiovascular system. When atrial fibrillation from preexisting conditions, is related to heart failure, strokes and blood clots, it stands to reason that the lack of enough necessary energetic minerals, such as sodium chloride, coupled with malnutrition could be the reason why blood clots happen or why people die from strokes and heart attacks [42]. Having enough nutrients and minerals could be the reason why some people survive heart attacks and strokes. If you have survived a heart attack or stroke from malnutrition and predispositions, you had enough electrolytes in your chloride channels, at that moment in time, to give you that extra push, the defibrillation. However, the next time, you may not be so lucky, if you do not change your ways. **Finally, Salt does not cause high blood pressure. It is the trigger of the immune system bringing up the salt in the body to energize the antidiuretic hormone which increases the blood flow in the kidneys to retain water. This saves the person from dehydration because the person was not drinking enough water. Salt is a person's rehydration insurance policy[96].** Could Salt backed by the necessary minerals, nutrition and acids save someone from dying from a heart attack? My research suggests it is very possible.

Salt, Mucus and Lungs.

I will go over mucus and antibodies in greater depth further on, in *Chapter 6 Mucus and Antibodies*, but this chapter is a good description of how Salt, antibodies and mucus work together. Salt is necessary to trigger the energy necessary to purge the stress from the body. For example, when the body gets exposed to an overabundance of antigen such as virus data or excess bacteria, minerals or hormones, antibodies get produced and released through mucus.

> *The major antibodies found on mucous membranes are secretory IgA, which function primarily by binding microorganisms and thereby preventing their contact with the host tissues [48]*

If you ever cried in your life and you tasted your tears and your nose is running with mucus, chances are your tears and mucus tasted salty. There's a reason why. **Salt is the energizing force to purge trauma such as stress and antigen from the body.** Crying is necessary to release emotions such as joy, sadness, grief and frustration [45]. I was taught never to hold onto emotions, but to let them out. Cancer comes from too many aggressive emotions being suppressed in the body causing negative mutations such as cancer [46]. Tears and mucus are salty because it is the body's balancing force releasing trauma and stress by the energy of the Salt and water as the carrier force.

> *The tear film is approximately 8–9μm thick and is comprised of 98.2% water and 1.8% solids. The three layers that make up the tear film are lipid, aqueous and mucous. The mucin layer is composed of high molecular glycoproteins, electrolytes, and water. It is secreted principally by the conjunctival goblet cells [47].*

Mucus and tears are a barometer measuring how much stress there is in the body and it needs to be released. When the body is constantly adjusting to its internal environment, as well as the external environment, mucus may happen, and tears may well up.

When a person lacks the electrolytes in a body that is riddled with weaknesses in their vital organs such as lungs, heart, brain, liver and kidneys, the body will have a hard time purging the antibodies within the mucus membrane. Therefore, people can die from pneumonia because they drown in their own fluids. For example, COVID-19 is a very new virus, triggering a type of acute respiratory disease, discovered late January 2020. The virus has been said to aggressively attack the lung tissue and other vital organs and potentially cause death [90]. The symptoms are shortness of breath and pressure on the lungs from the rapid accumulation of fluids, housing antibodies attacking the aggressive antigen, causing damage to precious lung tissue. People do not necessarily die from cancer, disease and chronic illness. They die from antibody accumulation agglutinating, causing blockages to the vital organs, as well as, the rapid replication of cancer cells triggering antibodies, attacking their vital organs. Antibody accumulation is triggered by the imbalances in the fatty acids, amino acids, prohormones and minerals. Then, the viruses, bacteria, fungi, protozoa, parasites and proteins all receive chemical messages to recycle the body back into the Earth again to start over again.

This is exactly why the Salt is a very important component of Jilly Juice along with the water, cabbage, kale, the fermentation time, temperature and ratios. This salty combination allows the body to absorb properly and release any excess acids, nutrition and minerals is paramount in continuous cellular regeneration which could contribute to indefinite life. The ability to open up the sodium and chloride channels and spark the energy necessary to allow the intelligence of the body to work the way it needs to, addressing all the issues of the body, is revolutionary.

CHAPTER 5

The Jilly Juice Recipe

The 3 Day Ferment and the 24-Hour Ferment:

<u>The 3 Day Ferment:</u>

Ingredients:

1. 1 Cups loosely packed chopped Cabbage (red or green) and/or Kale.
2. 2 Cups of Tap, Reverse Osmosis or Filtered Bottled Water (not distilled)
3. 1 Tablespoon of Table Salt (99% Iodized or Non-Iodized Sodium Chloride NaCl 1% Anti-Caking Agent, or no Anti-Caking Agent) <u>**NO SEA SALT OR MINERAL SALT OR CELL SALT OR PINK SALT OR BLACK SALT OR COLORED SALT**</u>

Directions:

1. Place the cabbage/kale, water and Salt together in a blender and puree. The finer the cabbage in the ferment, the easier it will be to drink.
2. Pour the mixture into your jar. The jar should appear 25% solids and 75% liquid after it settles. Until you become familiar with how much cabbage/kale needs to be used, it is best to let it settle a bit to judge the ratios, as you can adjust the ratio at this stage by adding either more pureed cabbage, or more brine (water & Salt), though there is no need for this to be a perfect ratio, it will

be drinkable either way, and you can just improve this with the next batch.
3. Cover the jar with an airtight lid. (If there is exposed metal in your lid, you may use a coffee filter placed between the jar and the lid in case the lids rust and are harder to open.) Glass jars with self-locking mechanisms and rubber grommets do not need coffee filters.
4. Let mixture stand at room temperature (ferment) for at least 3 days or more until consumed or store in refrigerator (around 65-72 degrees F). If you are in a colder climate, (less than 65 degrees in the house) leave out longer prior to putting it in the refrigerator. If you are in hot climate (10 degrees or more above the recommended temperature), you can leave it out or store in the refrigerator sooner, if you like it cold. Make sure you don't leave the jars in direct sunlight as heat does kill live active cultures. Keep the jars away from heat and flame and hot surfaces. You can shake, mix, stir or open the ferments at any time after the initial 3 days, however, it does not require burping.
5. After the 3 days (72 hours) or more has passed, the fermenting is completed. Gently stir the mixture and drink (or refrigerate for later use).
6. If you are storing your ferment in the refrigerator, it is recommended to stir it or turn it upside down, if you want to check for air leaks, every day or every few days, to keep any floating solids on the top saturated with the brine. This recipe can be stored forever.
7. DO NOT DILUTE AT ALL, unless you are just starting. YOU WANT A HIGH CONCENTRATION OF THIS FERMENT SO YOU CAN START FEELING THE UPGRADES.

The 24-Hour Ferment (subsequent batches):

This is the same as the 3 Day Ferment, except you are using your previous ferment as a "starter" so it will only need to ferment for 24 hours, since batches using "starter" (previously completed ferments) will be finished much faster.

Directions: Use a small portion of the last ferment as a starter to decrease the time necessary for the batch to ferment.

Approximately 1/4 - 1/2 Cup of previously made 3 Day Ferment per batch. (If you are using a gallon sized jar 1 Cup will be fine.)

1. Continue to fill the jar with the fresh pureed cabbage/kale, water and Salt as described for the 3 Day Ferment.
2. Let mixture stand at room temperature for 1 day (24 hours).
3. After 1 day (24 hours) has passed the fermenting is completed. Gently stir the mixture and drink (or refrigerate for later use).

*******Emergency Food Recipe for Low Sugar Issues and Weight Gain Intentions*

- This is only to be used in lieu of Candy while waiting for an emergency medical team, if they are available.
- Add 1 Tsp or more (as needed) of Regular Maple Syrup (Corn Syrup/High Fructose Corn/Fruit Syrup) to 1 Cup of fermented Jilly Juice.
- Drink

The Jilly Juice Protocol has no diet, per se. You will read more about that later. Instead of adding sugar to the recipe on the Jilly Juice Protocol, I decided to allow all foods on the protocol, and then you will listen to the indicators of your body, to see if that food is appropriate at the time. Some people do need carbohydrates, sugars and fermented cabbage juice together to balance out their biochemistry. While other people need to cut down on their intake of carbohydrates and sugars and bring in the sodium chloride, backed by cabbage, water, and probiotics. However, in extreme circumstances such as COVID 19, for example, and no access to quick medical help, the Jilly Juice recipe with Maple Syrup added to it after fermentation, is much better, if not very similar, to the IV Bags used in the intensive care units in hospitals. Extreme drops in blood sugars stemming from viral exposure can be deadly if you do not act quickly.

...unavailability of testing equipment should not delay treatment if hypoglycemia is suspected.[6] In the conscious

patient, the most practical treatment is the oral administration of a rapid-acting carbohydrate (TABLE 4) [94].

Shopping List for the Recipe.

a. Cabbage and/or kale
b. Tap Water, Filtered spring water (7ph), well water, reverse osmosis water,
c. White Table Salt or iodized Salt (99% Sodium Chloride 1% anti-caking agent)
d. Measuring cup
e. Tablespoon Salt per batch
f. Blender/Nutribullet/food processor/knife (not everyone has electricity)
g. Refrigerator
h. Large <u>glass</u> jars with <u>airtight</u> Lids
i. Coffee Filters if needed to as a barrier for bare metal lids if the Salt rusted the lids making it hard to open. Glass jar with rubber grommets and locking mechanism no need for coffee filters.

Other Items for JJ Used Topically, As Needed.

1. Eye dropper bottles with eye dropper
2. Douche bottles/Enema Bottles
3. Ace bandage/Saran wrap. Keep whole fermented cabbage leaves in place over concerned areas, if severe, see a Doctor.
4. Spray bottle for spraying ferment on skin/scalp for skin issues or just to be kind to your skin!
5. Syringe/Douche bottle for ferment enemas.
6. Gauze/cotton/cotton cloths (for soaking and applying on eyes or skin etc.)
7. Large Jar for fermenting whole cabbage leaves for your preexisting conditions
8. A dropper for ear drops
9. Nebulizer to nebulize the juice minus the solids

Choosing Your Jar(s).

The 2-cup base recipe will fit in a 1-pint jar (16 oz.) or be repeated to fit larger jars like 1-gallon jars or more. This can be any jar from a cleaned out recycled spaghetti sauce jar to a nice Mason jar (Ball jar). The important thing is that you have an airtight lid, and if your lid is uncoated metal (like the two-part Mason jar canning lid) you want to have a coffee filter between the lid and the jar. Plan for the amount you intend to start ingesting and the timing you need to continue the batch. It is probably best to begin with a quart sized jar (32 oz) which will fit 2 batches to begin. If you plan to begin more aggressively (more than 2 cups a day), you will obviously need more jars or larger jars, so this is a personal choice.

Cabbage and Kale.

Cabbage (green or purple) and/or Kale are another personal preference, and it may be one or the other, or any combination of the two. It can be freeze dried powder, frozen or fresh and does not have to be organic. One large head of cabbage yields about 2.5 gallons of juice, so purchase according to how much you choose to make and drink. I have many people asking me why I chose cabbage and kale instead of other vegetables. It was just by happenstance or accidental, yet strategic. Luckily, both of those vegetables are very dense in nutrition. I originally started using cucumbers to make pickles using the same recipe, but I could not yield enough juice to make it worthwhile. When I tried carrots, I ran into the same issues. I found cabbage and kale to be the easiest to yield large amounts of liquid and so chock full of nutrients there must be a correlation why the body repairs itself so quickly. The number of vitamins, minerals and nutrients in cruciferous vegetables, far outweighs fermenting a few other vegetables put together, and the cabbage and kale are the easiest to ferment. Plus, knowing how the Holistic fermentation community goes crazy on fermenting everything, I did not want people fermenting high sugary veggies or fruits because the sugars are enhanced during fermentation, and it feeds fungus and causes more antibody accumulation due to high acid imbalances. That is also why the protocol does not include any vinegars or fermented drinks like kombucha or apple cider vinegar, as a remedy. However, people will drink whatever they want, but if you do partake in the above, drink a lot of the Jilly Juice to balance the sugar acids and other acids.

Lactobacillus from Fermentation Using Cabbage and Kale.

Lactobacillus is one of nine strains of probiotics, or bacteria that reside in the guts [69]. It is a type of endospore highly resilient in aggressive environments and very hard to destroy and can be grown in all types of fermentation. *This is why you can shake your ferments or turn them upside down during fermentation.* Disinfectants, radiation, humidity and heat have a hard time destroying the spores, even if the bacteria are rendered chemically inert by aggressive elemental imbalances [67]. Nonetheless, lactobacillus is part of a family of probiotic bacteria you need to be able to function within biodiversity.

> *Probiotics are defined as live microorganisms, which when administered in adequate amounts, confer a health benefit on the host. Health benefits have mainly been demonstrated for specific probiotic strains of the following* genera: *lactobacillus, bifidobacterium, saccharomyces, enterococcus, streptococcus, pediococcus, leuconostoc, bacillus, escherichia coli [65].*

Balance is still the theme of Jilly Juice and balance also applies to all bacteria which reside in your gut. Different bacterial infections come from bacterial imbalances in the body such as streptococcus triggering strep throat [66]. You can also have imbalances in your lactic acid from the lactobacillus and other bacteria causing lactic acidosis, which may be overabundant in your body, hence electrolytes are used to keep the balance, mitigating hyponatremia. The Jilly Juice Protocol with the cabbage and kale, water and White Table Salt, allow a certain type of lactobacillus called *L plantarum*. *L plantarum* is the type of resilient endospore that also thrives in high salinity, just like the first life form of protein found to thrive in saltwater billions of years ago [68]. This is the sole reason why I have said that it is not necessary to drink massive amounts of kombucha, apple cider vinegar or elderberry syrup in reaction to disease. People are electrolyte deficient and the fermented vinegars and high sugar foods on low sodium chloride diets cause hyponatremic conditions causing Cancer, heart failure, pneumonia, and kidney failure.

The Salt.

It is important to use white iodized or non-iodized table Salt. It can be 99% sodium chloride and 1% anti-caking agent, which are types of minerals used, and it is not poisonous in the ratios of the food grade Salt. It is a mineral the body will be able to reconcile and absorb and release. The pink Himalayan Salt, cell salts, mineral (heavy metal) salts or sea salts have less sodium chloride, more heavy metals and is not as effective for what we are trying to do with the Jilly Juice. White Table Salt is the most powerful and energetic compound on this Earth.

The Water.

Water has been a huge debate the last 5-10 years or more because of all the mass media horror stories about what the cities and counties are putting in the public water supply. From fluoride to chlorine to lithium and heavy metals, the public water supply has been under fire for some time now. Water filters and reverse osmosis filtration systems have flooded the market to such an extent, one must wonder what is behind all this big business concerning the water supply. The kind of water used in my protocol is going to be whatever you deem is accessible in your situation, and tap water is optimal unless you are in Flint, Michigan with known water issues. The good news is that lacto-fermentation, using the White Table Salt and the cabbage and kale, controls all known pathogens such as excess mold/fungus or yeast. Fluoride and heavy metals have been highlighted in the Holistic community used as a fear mongering tactic to urge people to buy expensive water filtration systems. I suspect there is a business behind the fear mongering as I have seen people pay hundreds and hundreds of dollars for water filtration systems. Fluoride and heavy metals are needed minerals the body will be able to process backed by the energizing force of the White Table Salt found in Jilly Juice. All types of water, except alkaline water set higher than 7ph neutral or pond water, is acceptable. However, pond water you can boil first, and the Salt and lactobacillus in

THE EVOLUTION OF THE JILLY JUICE PROTOCOL

my recipe will also control bacteria and parasites in the water, since the recipe purges excess human parasites and excess fungus in the body. For this reason, some protocol users also use my recipe on their pets and plants with great results.

How to Correct Mistakes When Fermenting.

When you are first making the recipe, you may end up with way too much cabbage and the juice is not going to be liquid enough to get down. That's okay. When you are done fermenting and you're ready to drink, just add enough water and Salt so you can swallow it easily and get it down into your body. The next time you start to do your recipe, stop and let things settle when you're about halfway up the jar, and see how much there is water and Salt to cabbage. If you find that you have way more cabbage than water and Salt, then lay off the cabbage and just add the same ratios of water and Salt until you can even out the jar, so it looks 25/50. Let's say for example you forget to put the right amount of Salt and you are already in the middle of the second day of fermentation. Well just add the Salt, mix everything around and then ferment for the next 3 days or more or 24 hours or more, whichever fermentation process you are doing. Let's say you didn't add enough water. What I would do is put everything in a bigger jar, add the right ratios of water, and then ferment for the next 3 days or more or 24 hours or more relative to whatever process you are doing. You may see mold and yeast if you are using mineral salts not White Table Salt and I will discuss that in another section.

Mold.

Mold will only happen if your Salt is NOT pure White Table Salt. If you are using mineral Salt, mold thrives on the carbon chemical reaction of minerals [50] and the organic matter from cabbage and kale fermentation when it is exposed to oxygen.

> *Mold, fungus, lichens, algae or other similar substances can grow on the inside of Quartz and other rocks that are fractured [49].*
> *Quartzite Composition (minerals in the quartz)*

> *Quartzite consists almost entirely of silicon dioxide, SiO_2. If the purity is about 99% SiO_2, the rock is called orthoquartzite. Otherwise, quartzite commonly contains iron oxide and may contain trace amounts of the mineral's rutile, zircon, and magnetite. Quartzite may contain fossils [50].*

Yeast.

Yeast will happen when you are not using pure White Table Salt. It is like a white film or maybe a brownish color on the top of the exposed solids due to air leakage. The reasons why this may happen, is when you use the mineral (heavy metal) salts not on the protocol. Below is an excerpt of fermentation of sugars and alcohols encouraging yeast, which is not the point of Jilly Juice. In the beginning of the protocol, we accepted it as a possibility when fermenting, but now, it will not happen with White Table Salt, as much. There are still organic and inorganic compounds in the water, cabbage and kale. But we are still NOT using mineral (heavy metal) salts at all with the Jilly Juice Protocol. However, if you are still using up your mineral (heavy metal) salts, the potential for yeast and mold are still a possibility but not a big deal. Just mix and stir.

> *Nitrogen (YAN), vitamins (thiamine) and mineral salts (Mg, Zn) are essential for yeast activity. ... It stimulates yeast growth, speeds up fermentation and reduces production of SO2 binding compounds. Minerals are components of the yeast cell membrane and help maintain fermentation metabolism activities [51].*

This is not a big deal, if you happen to grow yeast with your ferments if you're still using mineral salts (remember, you have a balance of Yeast in your body). It will just taste and smell differently (possibly strong and unpleasant) and that is fine, just mix it with other better smelling and tasting batches. If you do not like the taste of a batch, you can still drink it if you choose, but do not use it for the next 24-Hour ferment or your next batch will taste very similar, like human replication from reproduction. Do you see that connection? Offspring take on similar characteristics from their parents. Just make a new batch. Make sure you mix and stir every time a batch is done before storing it. **Note: Fungal or Yeast infections come from lack of adequate number of electrolytes in the body. Imbalances in your microbiome is like imbalances in your ferments. Salt, an electrolyte, is the balancing force controlling yeast and fungal growth.**

Storage.

You can store this juice almost forever. Just make sure everything is below the brine and you mix and check for mold, if you are using mineral (heavy metal) salts because any exposed pieces, even in a sealed environment can still mold while your drink is still fermenting, even in the refrigerator. If you stick to white table Salt, you will not have a major problem with mold or yeast.

Botulism in canning versus lactic fermentation and mold and yeast.

Botulisms are bacteria that get into the container when someone is trying to preserve a vegetable and a fruit. Oxygen and heavy metals also, foster that environment. Botulism happens when all those pathogenic bacteria swell the contents of the can, rendering it poisonous to humans. The reason why botulism is a fear in the canning community, is because the canning process does not create lactobacillus, and it does not have the right amount of Salt to render pathogenic bacteria chemically inert. So, there is no fear of botulism when you're doing lacto-fermentation because there is no heat applied.

Drinking the Jilly Juice.

Since I changed the Salt from the pink Himalayan Salt chock full of heavy metals also known as "trace minerals," to white table Salt, the energy behind the Jilly Juice will be far greater. You will not have to drink as much to get the benefit. The "gallon a day" that was previously admonished as unappealing, will not be necessary. Realistically, only a few people on the Jilly Juice claimed they were drinking a gallon a day and received results. Just go slow, at your pace, and drink more as you feel your body start to feel and upgrade. As stated in previous chapters, the pain process is the upgrading process and you will manage that process on your own or with your doctor.

You also need to be prepared for the fact that this ferment may at first, smell and taste objectionable when you first start using it. This improves over time as you upgrade. You will want to have a glass of nice cool water or a shot of fruit juice on hand to chase the taste with, as well as to drink after the juice. Many people also have a plate or bowl of fresh fruit (watermelon or grapes are great for this) on hand to chase the juice with between sips. After you have consumed the Jilly Juice, you will follow with an equal amount (or more) of water. Afterward, listen to your body and drink water as your thirst dictates, but do not try to go beyond that and overdo the water without thirst.

Purging is the waterfalls of poop coming out of your behind after you drink my recipe quickly in a short amount of time as well as mucus or a runny nose. It is a type of non-dehydrative autophagy [91], or an activation of the colon to release the waste. (Remember, there are electrolytes in the Jilly Juice). I will discuss the poop coming out your behind called Waterfalls, in the next chapter.

CHAPTER 6

What to Expect with Jilly Juice and How to Implement

Silk Road or the Alimentary Canal.

Silk Road or Silk Route is very similar to the structures and intentions of the alimentary canal.

> *Silk Road, also called Silk Route, ancient trade route, linking China with the West, that carried goods and ideas between the two great civilizations of Rome and China. [77].*

The analogy is quite appropriate, because humanity improved significantly, when able to share new revolutionary ideas and strategic goods, to make life easier during the 15th and early 16th centuries, until it subsequently ended in the 19th century [78]. Despite the shutdown of the original Silk Road, the ideas live on in a figurative way when it comes to global trade. Global imports and exports help struggling economies become a significant player in the world market and therefore lives improve from the currency they receive from their goods and services.

This is not unlike the alimentary canal which is a long tube connecting the mouth and the anus together with many organs and systems interwoven into the canal. Each system and organ are interdependent on the other, therefore, if one organ or system fails, they all will either fail or go into a rapid or slow decline relative to the methodologies applied [79][80]. What would make the alimentary canal fail to give the human access to its maximum potential? The answer is, predispositions, preexisting conditions and anomalies in the genetics also called epigenetics. Epigenetics, also known as mutations, can evolve or devolve a human based upon how strong or weak the human is. However, currently humanity is suffering from chronic to occasional conditions getting progressively worse as the years go by, also called aging, which is covered in *Chapter 3 Aging, Reproduction and Death*. The process to potentially counter the aging process is understanding how to apply the Jilly Juice with an understanding antibodies are in mucus, feces and urine and how they must leave the body in order to bring your internal ecosystem back into balance.

Mucus and Antibodies/Entities.

If excess antibodies/entities are found in bodily fluids such as, sweat, feces, breast milk, tears, urine, blood, semen, reproductive fluids, saliva and mucus [85], then, mucus is a data pack of antibodies, Salt, water and protein and various types of dead leukocytes found in the abovementioned delivery systems [86]. This is the body's way of recalibrating when exposed to a new or excess bacterium, virus, protozoa, fungi, protein, parasite or mineral. Under normal circumstances, overabundance of the above trigger the mucus to develop, then the excess gets released. On the other hand, if stagnancy occurs, the antibodies will agglutinate and then reinfection occurs. A well-functioning system with adequate number of electrolytes or Salt would be able to release the excess antibodies in mucus that do get created. However, all aging bodies taking on antigen triggering antibodies have problems recalibrating their system. Therefore, symptoms appear when the body is exposed to new entities or needs to release excess entities. For example, some people get symptoms from vaccines, which is the body's way of adapting and releasing antibodies. Not everyone gets symptoms from new exposures, however, it is relative to how weak or strong their body and immune system are. The difference is in how aggressive the person's symptoms are. Once the body adapts to the new environment, the symptoms disappear. Sometimes, people's symptoms from the new exposures never disappear. That is called disease, or Cancer. It is like your body must adjust to the new world of entities on their way in, and then revisit the old world (experiences, traumas, pain) of antibodies on their way out. And if you suffer Cancer, disease and chronic illness, your body is exhibiting maladaptive traits causing you to react to the old antibodies and new antibodies. Waterfalls, inducing autophagy by activating an internal colonic on the Jilly Juice Protocol, will help a person transition and adapt to their environment easier once they release the antibodies their bodies have held onto for years.

IgA, IgG and IgM are faeces were quantified by single radial immunodiffusion using extracts of freeze-dried faeces. IgA in small specimens of faeces seemed to mirror the total amount of IgA secreted into the gut at the time of sampling [53].

Scheduling Your Waterfalls.

Jilly Juice is a powerful force of nutrition backed by the energizing force of the white table Salt. Remember, before you drink Jilly Juice, it will clean out your colon, also known as autophagy. So, you must plan and then learn how to gauge when to induce autophagy. Autophagy is the body's ability to purge out the excess antibodies and waste material that cause destruction to precious tissues in the 11 different systems. [91]

Earlier in the book, I established why people die. It is from acquiring too many antibodies with a very stagnant release rate; thus, the antibodies clog up the arteries and capillaries and block oxygen getting to the heart, brain and lungs. These antibodies also induce abnormal cell replication called Cancer, triggering more antibodies. Jilly Juice is cabbage, kale, water and white table Salt fermented down to a predigested state, like mother's milk or regurgitated baby bird food. When a person drinks this, the cells in the digestive system absorb the nutrients. Upon absorption, the sodium and chloride channels in the cells and motor neurons are buzzing with activity taking all the different fatty acids, amino acids, prohormones and minerals and delivering them to their proper places, and the excess is pushed out through the digestive tract. The body also triggers apoptosis, a programmed cell death [54], and autophagy which is why you see the rapid release of dysfunctional cells, such as rotting teeth and excessive non-dehydrative defecation occurs that sometimes feels like waterfalls. The body finally wakes up and can now work correctly.

There have been concerns with the amount of Salt intake with the Jilly Juice, but it is not just saltwater or only Salt. The Jilly Juice is full of electrolytes, probiotics and micro and macro nutrition, fermented down to a predigested state, and it is very rehydrating, since we also drink water when we are thirsty. It is a synergistic protocol that is completely aligned with biodiversity and biochemistry.

> *Electrolytes interact with each other and the cells in the tissues, nerves, and muscles. A balance of different electrolytes is vital for healthy function. They regulate nerve and muscle function, hydrate the body, balance blood acidity and pressure, and help rebuild damaged tissue [52].*

Using Western Medicine and Drinking Jilly Juice With Predispositions.

People on the Jilly Juice Protocol came into the fold with predispositions. These predispositions are triggered by the antibodies causing issues in their 11 different systems, and so people experience all sorts of symptoms when they are sick, as the body tries to upgrade. Everyone, who comes into the protocol, already exhibit one or more of the conditions listed below. Some are experiencing these preexisting conditions now, or may experience them later, due to predispositions coming to surface from antibodies being released from autophagy and apoptosis:

- Acne
- Allergy symptoms
- Ankle, swollen from past sprain
- Anxiety
- Appetite loss
- Back pain
- Barfing, sometimes worms/parasites
- Bloating
- Burping
- Chest congestion

- Chilled feeling
- Cold hands and feet
- Constipation
- Coughing, maybe with green phlegm
- Cystic acne recurrence
- Diarrhea
- Dizziness
- Dry mouth
- Dry skin
- Eye twitch
- Face burning feeling
- Face red
- Farting/gas
- Fatigue/exhaustion
- Fingers tingling
- Flu type symptoms
- Foggy feeling
- Frequent urination
- Growing pains in kids
- Gum/root pain
- Gums burning
- Headache
- Heart palpitations
- Heart racing
- Heartburn
- Hemorrhoids
- Herpes outbreak
- Hot flashes
- Hunger pains/growling stomach
- Increased libido
- Intense emotions
- Itchy skin, scalp, ears, eyes
- Joint pain
- Joint swelling
- Leg Cramps
- Liver pain right side of torso

- Lucid dreams
- Lymph node swelling/pain
- Metal taste in mouth
- Migraines
- Mild chest pain
- Missing organs, limbs, digits, skin grafts, implants
- Mucus from ears
- Mucus in throat and nose
- Muscle soreness
- Nausea
- Neck pain
- Ovary pain
- Panic attacks
- Past pain reoccurring for short time
- Pooping parasites
- Rashes
- Runny nose
- Sinus infection
- Sinus pain/pressure
- Sleeplessness
- Sore throat
- Stuffy nose
- Sugar cravings
- Swollen face and eyes
- Swollen hands
- Swollen lymph nodes
- Thirst
- Thrush/white tongue
- Urinary tract infection
- Uterine, sharp pain
- Vomiting
- Weight loss
- Wrist pain
- Zits, expelling yellow/white beads

The list above are some examples of antibodies/entities exacerbating your current systems, causing symptoms and it is up to you to upgrade the weaknesses and purge them out. Some of these antibodies/entities are from past traumas that have been suppressed from years of therapies and drugs. Other antibodies, along with overabundant entities from your microbiome, are right at the surface shedding continuously, because they are so prevalent. Either way, you MUST deal with these antibodies/entities being brought to surface and then eventually purged. If not, the antibodies/entities will agglutinate or multiply and inhibit proper healthy cell replication causing vital organs to shut down. These antibodies/entities get released from the body through your urine, feces, mucus and all exit points relative to your infections and weaknesses. They could be at the surface of your skin itching or they could feel like pain in parts of your body like dull aches or sharp pains. No matter what, if you feel your issues and predispositions are unmanageable, always see a doctor to stabilize you at your comfort level. Never ever stop drinking Jilly Juice. In the future, it is expected that once you have expelled the excess antibodies/entities and allowed deep cellular regeneration, your adaptation process will get easier and easier, despite the changes in the environment. You will always experience periods of adjustment if your environment become aggressive or the season changes. However, those on Jilly Juice, will have an easier time over those who are not.

Figure 1.
[81]

All the information below, is merely a snapshot of what some people did, while managing their preexisting conditions, in conjunction with Jilly Juice, their prescription meds and doctor's approval.

12 Different Systems	System Functions	Organs Associated	Upgrading Symptoms	Using My Juice
1. Skeletal System	Bones are the framework of the body made up of proteins, cells, joints, fibers and minerals. New blood cells are produced by the bone marrow and it is the body's warehouse of calcium, iron and energy in the form of fat.	Bone/Ligaments/ Joints Tendons Cartilage	Preexisting Conditions, such as: bones aches from upgrading and growing and shifting, pain from blunt force trauma	Spray bottle (for spraying ferment on skin/scalp for rashes or just to be kind to your skin! You can also ferment whole cabbage leaves in lots of Juice and use saran wrap or an ace bandage and wrap parts of the body with it and soak it for a few hours
2. Muscular System	There about 700 muscles that make up half the person's body weight made up of nerves, blood vessels, tendons and skeletal muscle tissues.	Muscle Tissues throughout the body.	Preexisting Conditions, such as: Muscle soreness and swelling and pain. This may happen all over the body or parts of body, joint pain, leg cramps, weakness, inflammation, skin rashes,	Spray bottle (for spraying ferment on skin/scalp for rashes or just to be kind to your skin!

3. Cardiovascular System	This system consists of the heart, which is a muscle, pumping blood throughout the body using blood vessels transporting oxygen, nutrients, hormones and cellular waste.	Heart Arteries Blood Vessels Capillaries Veins	Preexisting Conditions, such as: heart palpitations, heart racing, mild chest pains, head rush, dizziness	Keep Drinking the Juice, and get whatever tests done to give you peace of mind.
4. Digestive System	This is a group of organs working symbiotically together converting food into energy, as well as basic nutrients to feed the entire body. This system filters out the waste allowing for a more effective absorption.	Mouth Esophagus Stomach Small Intestine Large Intestine Rectum/Liver/Gall Bladder Appendix Pancreas	Preexisting Conditions such as: Digestive issues, throwing up worms and parasites, nausea, appetite loss, farting, gas, cravings or hunger pains, stomach gurgling, diarrhea, constipation, stomach pain, cramps, pooping up worms and parasites. Mouth and gum, root pain. sugar and carbs cravings, liver pain, thirst, dry mouth, thirst, thrush on tongue, swollen, tonsils, metal taste in mouth	Keep Drinking the Juice and flood your system with my Juice in a short amount of time. The Goal to experience waterfalls of poop leaving your system. You will not be dehydrated, just keep drinking water if you are thirsty.

THE EVOLUTION OF THE JILLY JUICE PROTOCOL

5. Endocrine System	**All the glands that produce the hormones in your body propelled by the nervous system makes up the Endocrine System.**	Hypothalamus. Pituitary gland. Thyroid. Parathyroid's. Adrenal glands. Pineal body. Reproductive glands (which include the ovaries and testes) Pancreas.	Preexisting Conditions, such as: Cold and hot feeling, cold hands and feet, anxiety, ovary pain, testicular pain, sleepiness, fatigue, feelings of happiness, sadness and depression relative to past traumatic experiences, intense emotions, sleeplessness, manic feeling, eye twitch	Keep drinking the JJ.
6. Nervous System	**The sensory organs, brain, the spine, the nerves and all the organs communicating, is the job of the nervous system.**	Brain Spinal Cord Nerves	Preexisting Conditions, such as: Headaches and tingling of the skin and panic attacks. Foggy feeling, feeling like you are dissociated, not there. Swelling of face and eyes, eye pain, itchy eyes, dizziness, lucid dreaming, intense dreams, migraines,	Spray bottle (for spraying ferment on skin/scalp for rashes or just to be kind to your skin!

7. Respiratory System	Oxygen is what keeps the cells in the human body alive. This system provides oxygen to the cells in the body, removing the carbon dioxide which is deadly to the body if allowed to accumulate [95].	Lungs and Nose and throat	Preexisting Conditions, such as: Mucus in the ear, nose, throat, ear. Allergy symptoms, bloating/burping, heartburn, sinus pain and pressure, sore throat, coughing up green phlegm and cough, and stuffy nose,	Consult your doctor or try nebulizing the JJ without the solids.
8. Immune/Lymphatic System	These two systems are linked together physiologically with the body's defense system against infectious from excess viruses, bacteria, fungi and parasites proteins, and protozoa.	The Gut and Digestive System	Preexisting Conditions, such as: Lymph nodes swelling, infections, fever	Keep Drinking the Juice and stay with the protocol as the swelling will go down.
9. Urinary System	This is a system of organs that filter the blood from waste to produce urine.	Urinary Tract for both men and women	Preexisting Conditions, such as: Frequent urination, urinary tract infections, smelly urine, copious amounts of urine as the kidneys upgrade, mucus in the urine, urine different colors	Keep Drinking the Juice or use the liquid syringe with the Juice up there in men or women or use the Juice in the belly button using a cotton ball to keep in place

10. Female Reproductive System	This system not only supplies the eggs, but it houses the space or uterus for a baby to develop during a 9-month gestation period by the transportation of sperm from the male. This process is supported by the transportation of the gametes producing a sex hormone. This system is located at the apex of the leg called the vulva and travels inside up the birth canal towards the pelvis, and branches off into two sets of ovaries and fallopian tubes, and then the female hormones signal the lactation process to develop in the breast area.	Labia and birth canal, ovaries, uterus, vulva, cervix	Preexisting Conditions, such as: Fungal infections, pain or pressure in the cervix and uterus, bleeding, mucus, green or yellow discharge, fishy smell, yeasty smell, cramping, herpes outbreaks, hot flashes, increased libido, sharp uterine pain,	Syringe/Douche Bottle (for ferment enemas) and just filter out the chunks of the ferment and use the juice to douche and spray below the waistline.

11. Male Reproductive System	With several organs working together to produce male gamete sex hormones that eventually come out into semen and little sperm fertilizing the egg when given permission by the female.	Penis, testicles, Sperm	Preexisting Conditions, such as: Fungus outbreak, testicular pain, urinary tract infection,	Spray bottle (for spraying ferment on skin/scalp for skin issues or just to be kind to your skin! You can also ferment whole cabbage leaves in lots of Juice and use saran wrap or an ace bandage and wrap parts of the body with it and soak it for a few hours
12. Integumentary System	This system is the first line of defense with the skin cross section: the hair, nails, exocrine system such as the sweat glands, sebaceous glands in the hair and skin, and it protects the body from UV light, chemicals and physical damage.	Hair, Skin, Nails, Scalp,	Preexisting Conditions, such as: Cystic Acne recurrence, dry skin, face red, zits expelling yellow and white beads, itchy skin, scalp, face, swelling of the face and eyes, hands and feet, face burning feeling, tingling feeling all over, weight loss and bloating	Spray bottle (for spraying ferment on skin/scalp for skin issues or just to be kind to your skin! You can also ferment whole cabbage leaves in lots of Juice and use saran wrap or an ace bandage and wrap parts of the body with it and soak it for a few hours

CHAPTER 7

To (Die)t or Not to (Die)t

The Food Supply and Jilly Juice.

My original protocol was acutely aware of how all types of food affect different people and their imbalanced biochemistry. To make a universal declaration that something is healthy or unhealthy, is a type of projection of someone's perception of what is healthy based upon their personal belief system. It does not mean it is correct or even appropriate. When doctors, naturopaths or homeopaths declare certain foods as poison or toxic, they have taken the adverse reactions from certain foods from most of their clients and made assertions. From these assertions, they made a correlation equals causation type of scenario, and then integrated those correlations of certain foods triggering inflammation, into their health regiment protocols and belief system. For example, there is a popular notion that meat is unhealthy and should be eradicated from the diet. Meat is made up of fatty acids, amino acids, prohormones and minerals and it is a very advanced source of nutrition. However, those with acid imbalances and a stagnated digestive system, may have a hard time processing red meat. Then, these perceptions of what is healthy or unhealthy become part of the health and wellness landscape and popularized and it becomes a type of "truth." It does not mean it is the truth, but it became a popular belief system enacted as if it were a truth.

Other popular food items demonized by those with imbalances, are Salt and sugar. I have covered the importance of Salt earlier on, please refer to *Chapter 4 Geopolitics, Jilly Juice and Indefinite Life.* Salt is necessary in assisting the body to hold onto water and energize the cells and organs to properly function. It is a crystal, and water soluble just like sugar, which also works the same with a similar and different functions. Salt is also a source of energy for the body to be able to function and trigger electrical impulses, like motor neurons, and Salt keeps all the systems working to ultimate capacity. Sugar and Salt are extremely necessary for the body to function, but we need to get past the myths of sugar before we can dispel the controversy around sugar in all its derivatives.

Sugar.

Sugar has been a source of controversy in the media, especially within all the health and wellness groups. When I was researching on the Internet, looking for "benefits of sugar," I kept seeing headlines like, "The Dangers of Too Much Sugar", or "Sugar Causes Cancer", and so on. Article after article after article kept repeating the same mantra how dangerous sugar is. It reminded me of my discovery of how often Salt is demonized. Sugar is a compound made up of three elements, carbon, hydrogen and oxygen [56]. When the body has a metabolic disorder, the sugar gets stored into the body, called fat [57]. These fat cells are made up of triglycerides, which are at least 3 fatty acids and glycerol, a component of sugar [59]. The fat gets stored for later use. However, if the body does not move around enough to burn the fat or the body's biochemistry is imbalanced, more fat from an imbalanced diet is stored [58].

> *Glucose travels to the cells of the body where it is converted to energy & used to carry out various functions such as muscle contraction & temperature regulation. While some organs can also use protein and fat for energy, red blood cells and the brain exclusively use glucose for energy, so a certain amount of carbohydrate intake is necessary for normal brain and bodily function [55].*

Some people in the health and wellness world know that some form of sugar is needed. It has been professed that fructose sugar is far better over dietary sugars and vice versa. Nevertheless, their practices of demonization of one type of sugar over another, fails to surprise me. It is all a marketing agenda. However, science and peer reviewed studies have proven in small experimental circumstances that all types of sugars, in whatever form, are not bad for you, unless you already have metabolic imbalances or preexisting conditions.

> *It has been postulated that dietary sugar consumption contributes to increased inflammatory processes in humans, and that this may be specific to fructose (alone, in sucrose or in high-fructose corn syrup (HFCS)). .... the overall findings, as collectively analyzed by a meta-analysis, do not support the hypothesis that dietary fructose (alone or in HFCS) is more detrimental with respect to subclinical inflammation than dietary glucose or sucrose [82].*

Sugars, dietary sugars, sugar substitutes, organic sugars, processed sugars and all types of sugars are made up of compounds. They are made up of different conglomerations of carbon, hydrogen and oxygen. You might have other elements added to the sugars based upon specific dietary guidelines in the weight loss world or disease management world. The molecular differences between how much carbon, hydrogen and oxygen will only effect those who already have trouble balancing their biochemistry. Therefore, even aspartame, a sugar substitute, is not necessarily bad. It has a very similar compound to sugar, but nitrogen is added with a slightly different molecular structure [60]. Every food can be broken down to an elemental state making up compounds, and the effects are based upon how your biochemistry resolves the compounds you bring into your body.

Sugar and Salt and the Jilly Juice Protocol.

Salt, sugar and movement are a form of metabolic examples of burning energy. All three need to be balanced relative to the constituents of biochemistry and biodiversity. Chapter 5 and 6 describe the metabolic energy of the Salt in the Jilly Juice, called waterfalls, inducing autophagy. This is how excess water, acids, carbon, hydrogen, minerals, hormones get released as well as through breathing. The energy burned in exhaling carbon dioxide is also releasing excess fat in the body [61]. Some people turn to forms of exercise to burn fat, however, the build up of too much lactic acid or triggering lactic acidosis causes more metabolic imbalances [62]. Too much exercise, and a diet low in glucose and sodium chloride, also known as electrolyte imbalances, will cause the body to go into hyponatremia and then trigger heart failure, liver failure and other electrolyte imbalance diseases.

> *Hyponatremia reflects an excess of total body water (TBW) relative to total body sodium content. Because total body sodium content is reflected by ECF volume status, hyponatremia must be considered along with status of the ECF volume: hypovolemia, euvolemia, and hypervolemia (see Table: Principal Causes of Hyponatremia) [76].*

Conversely, on the flip side, my critics have used the argument of hypernatremia, when the body has too much Salt and not enough water [63]. Drink water on the protocol, drink water when you are thirsty, and the problem is solved. My critics have also used the argument that the waterfalls, the colon activation with the Jilly Juice, is the same thing as diarrhea. Not true. Diarrhea is when the body utilizes all the available fluids in the body to purge out excess fatty acids, amino acids, prohormones, minerals, fungus, viruses, bacteria, protozoa, parasites, and proteins. The person becomes depleted and dehydrated from lack of electrolytes, hence the fluids in the saline and glucose IV bags are a common way to stabilize people suffering from complications of dehydration from the flu [64]. Jilly Juice colon activation, is when the body is utilizing the electrolytes you are bringing into the body with the fermented cabbage and kale, using white table Salt and water, then stores any extra to be used as needed, triggering the upgrading process of the Body, Mind and Spirit.

Mucus and the Food Supply.

I noticed early in the protocol that my body was very sensitive to different foods based upon the make up of my biochemistry at the time of ingesting.

For example, I would eat a hamburger and fries and then immediately go into a major mucus attack. My nose became stuffy and my body felt like it was coming down with a cold right after eating that hamburger and fries. It puzzled me until I understood the role of the mucus as a barometer showing how well my body was adapting or not adapting to my environment and what I was ingesting. Since our biochemistry is made up of fatty acids, amino acids, prohormones and minerals, and I had not released the excess at that point, certain foods would trigger antibodies causing symptoms. Later, I was able to eat the same food and not trigger antibody accumulation, because my body was so well balanced, that it was able to utilize the nutrients in the hamburger and fries and release the excess strategically and efficiently. This same scenario needs to be applied to anyone doing the Jilly Juice Protocol. Pay attention to how foods, not just Jilly Juice, will affect you. If you have been diagnosed by a doctor with a food allergy, not just him/her say, "Stay away from this food or that food", but clinically diagnosed from a doctor, please listen to your doctor and follow your doctor's diet plan. If you are on prescription drugs, medications, or over the counter drugs, please follow your doctor's diet plan and recommendations. Jilly Juice is a probiotic paired with the correct elements. You will eventually learn how to balance out your own choices and your doctor's recommendations. Jilly Juice will cause you to feel an upgrade to your body with the correct chemistry of electrolytes, minerals, water and nutrients and it has the beneficial bacteria that is resilient in high salinity and aggressive environments.

Mucoid Plaque, Mucus and Jilly Juice.

You may experience releasing mucoid plaque from the activation of your colon using Jilly Juice. When the body is imbalanced in its electrolytes, people tend to hold onto waste in their body, hence lymphatic and digestive infections happen. Again, infection comes from an imbalanced microbiome causing rapid antibody proteins to develop as a balancing force until agglutination or reinfection occurs. The ability to release the excess entities in your microbiome, fatty acids, amino acids, prohormones and minerals wrapped in mucus, is paramount. If the body is not able to release the excess, the body either wraps the foreign objects in chondrocytes (cartilage) embedded into the body, or mucoid plaque is created to keep the excess from being absorbed into the body [70][71]. Additionally, you will also be releasing mucus after drinking Jilly Juice, because the body is now activating the release of the excess fatty acids, amino acids, prohormones, minerals, virus data, fungi, protozoa, parasites, proteins and bacteria. All of which are simplified into a chemical form called antigen triggering the formation of antibodies. If these antibodies/entities do not get released, the antibodies agglutinate, the entities multiply and overwhelm the body, and reinfection occurs within the body.

To diet or not to diet will always be the questions for people unaware of how to manipulate their own biochemistry to their advantage. It is easier for many to simply avoid foods or eat recommended foods, rather than pay attention to their own internal indicators. I suppose if a person is functioning under a haze of drugs, alcohol and sex, it is very hard to even recognize indicators. However, those indicators are there and mischaracterized. If society learned how to recognize mucus as an indicator, the body is releasing the excess, we could see people evolve faster to a more advanced life form. Mucus on the Jilly Juice is the body purging out the excess, and mucus from a specific food is the body purging out the excess. You need both the food and the Jilly Juice, but the one to give up, temporarily, is the food that is giving you excess mucus. The Jilly Juice will always be the protocol to help regulate your biochemistry, so you are aware of your body's indicators. And then eventually, you can reintroduce foods that used to cause you excess mucus, back to your body. That is the beauty of Jilly Juice!!

CHAPTER 8

Jilly Juice, Unintended Benefits, Plants and Animals

Unintended Benefits of Jilly Juice.

When I first created the Jilly Juice Protocol, I had specific symptoms I needed to cure. The main one was PMDD or premenstrual dysphoric disorder. It is a more pronounced form of premenstrual syndrome. They were very severe hormonal imbalances once a month that used to get in the way of my daily life. I had to plan out my life to make room for these fluctuations and down time. It was very miserable. You can see my focus was more on the body and I was not considering the mind and the spirit as part of that equation. Lo and behold, after a brief stint to Portugal, I noticed my mind and spirit started to become quite clear. I was not as reactive and triggered, and even more calm as time went on during the protocol. I stopped looping in traumas that used to come up for me at weird times and I became more self-aware. I started to see the connections to everything in the Universe, the body and in our society. I started to notice trends and patterns in relationships and stopped trying to force square pegs into round holes. I gave myself permission to start, stop and improve relationships. I learned how to apply boundaries where there were none and give space for growth in my community, Body, Mind and Spirit.

When a person first embarks on the Jilly Juice Protocol, they will have specific goals and dreams limited by their preexisting conditions and biochemistry at the time. Once a person stays on the protocol and applies it appropriately for their lifestyle, potentially, they will experience an expansion of their consciousness and stop plateauing in life. Therefore, it is hard to give people an answer when they ask what the protocol will do for them. More to the point, what is the protocol doing for you? You tell us, the world, how the change in your biochemistry is affecting your finances, work/life balance, your preexisting conditions. Then, we can have a conversation. The beauty of the Jilly Juice Protocol is to have no expectations, just like a plant. Plants respond exactly to what is in their environment. They do not make up stories, or reasons or definitions. They experience adaptation, death and rebirth at the micro level and the macro level. Just like a human. The only difference is Jilly Juice is encouraging humans to experience death at the micro level that allow for rebirth at the micro level, so the macro level still stays intact. Conversely, unless plants are under the influence of the Jilly Juice, they will experience adaptation, death and rebirth at both the micro and macro level.

Plants.

Plants are made up of fatty acids, amino acids, prohormones and minerals and they will get benefit from the Jilly Juice. You might need to dilute in water relative to the size of the plant. Yes, Jilly Juice is for all of biodiversity [74].

Animals.

Animals are also included in the kingdom of biodiversity. They also have very similar biochemistry to humans. Like anything, it is all about balance. All biodiversity dies from is the lack of continuous proper chemistry applied to their biochemistry. Animals suffer the same types of diseases humans do and they also experience imbalances in their fatty acids, amino acids, prohormones and minerals [75]. What if we applied the same rules of Jilly Juice to all farm animals and pets applied in appropriate amounts relative to size and lifestyle? We could keep our farm animals and pets for a very long time. Longer than the current life expectancy.

CHAPTER 9

The Kind of People Who Do the Jilly Juice

The Antibiotic/Probiotic Method.

The Holistic and Allopathic world are full of the people who apply aggressive antibiotics or aggressive probiotics to an imbalance in their biochemistry causing eventual cancer, disease and chronic illness. The issue with this methodology is your body is made up of biodiversity comprising of viruses, fungi, bacteria, protozoa, parasites, and proteins. They all serve a specific function mentioned in my prior chapters and to apply aggressive condensed ingredients with antibiotics or anti-life agents, you are harming yourself and then will eventually kill yourself over time. Conversely, applying too many pure probiotics without the proper electrolyte balance, will cause lactic acidosis [93]. One good example of the psychology behind this type of thought process is called Pari-Mutuel betting in the horse racing world. The odds are determined by the bettors [73]. The more the public bets for a "cure," which is temporary, using strictly antibiotics or pure forms of probiotics, the less the payout in money or in longevity of life. This is how the odds are made for horse racing. The more people bet on a single horse, the lower the rewards. The winnings are divided among the winners, in horse racing and the investments in the cures will make them more accessible and acceptable and people become dependent and tunneled on "cures." It is like the pendulum keeps swinging to one side or the other, but never stays in the middle. Another example would be someone who eats an alkaline or acidic diet based upon their nutritional deficiencies. The body does not need to be too alkaline/basic or too acidic, but more of a neutral pH balance [72]. What it all comes down to is the Salt ratios in the Jilly Juice is what makes the Jilly Juice Protocol not too acidic, not too alkaline and just the right balance of minerals, hormones and acids. This also translates within the body and then the intelligence of the body kicks in and starts regulating, recalibrating and balancing. Mucus, autophagy and apoptosis happen at a more accelerated rate, then people start upgrading their body regenerating cells with eventually never having to revisit their issues again.

Investing in Jilly Juice Is Like Bull/Bear Market on Wall Street.

Ever since 2016, I had so many different types of people come into the protocol, explore it, do it for a short time, then leave it. I also have people who have been with me ever since the beginning still doing the protocol and adapting to the changes and evolution of the protocol and me. I noticed a very interesting trend of people who start the protocol. It seems the people who implement the protocol right away, are those who have exhausted all resources and their back is against the wall. They literally have nothing else to turn to. Or, what they have been turning to has not worked and they are on the hunt, again, for a new protocol. The term buys low, sells high are those types of people who do the protocol. They are at their lowest in Body, Mind and Spirit and have nothing to lose. They know the only way is up at this point. Buying in a bear market with falling stock prices can be a goldmine if you can afford to lose your principal if the company goes belly up, which means you better have something on reserve. Of course, it is a gamble, but an educated gamble if you have done your research. Not unlike Jilly Juice. Given all controversy around Salt and the Jilly Juice Protocol, it can be quite a gamble for some who are not wholly prepared with certain timely expectations. It is not so much of a gamble for others who have done their research and are ready for the change in their biochemistry. If the only way is up, then an investor will surely make up for all the losses they ever had, prior to the Jilly Juice. On the flip side, those who are already flying high in Body, Mind and Spirit and in their health will not see a reason to invest in Jilly Juice until their body starts to degrade, or the market stock prices start to fall. This type of person is exhibiting bullish market tendencies and most likely will not entertain Jilly Juice. Why change their biochemistry if it is giving them excellent dividends now? However, hopefully, the Bullish Market type of individual will save enough for their rainy day so they can take the time to upgrade their body and go through the process of colon activation and adapting to the new environment of Jilly Juice. The Jilly Juice crowd does not want to be those who are a flash in the pan, with a limited life span.

Babies, Pregnant Mothers.

I have had many questions regarding whether the Jilly Juice is safe for pregnant mothers and their babies. Of course, it is safe. Jilly Juice is food. Like any food, eat in moderation, or feed in moderation and always listen to your doctor or nurse practitioner when it comes to neonatal and prenatal care. All of biodiversity needs fatty acids, amino acids, prohormones and minerals. Death comes from the final transfer of energy of life, due to lack of combustion from the proper chemical processes, comprising of the proper balance of electrolytes, hormones, and acids.

CONCLUSION

Jilly Juice Trifecta of Upgrading

Elements, Biodiversity, and Biochemistry.

We have established the body is made up of all of biodiversity and elements giving off different balances of biochemistry and your personal microbiome. Imbalances in your microbiome made up of viruses, bacteria, parasite, proteins, fungi and protozoa, cause infections triggering antibody production. The air, food, water and Earth are all made up of the same constituents of biodiversity in your microbiome. They all give off a form of biochemistry made up of fatty acids, amino acids, prohormones and minerals of which each entity will have very specific balances relative to their purposes. The application of aggressive chemicals in the remedies and immunotherapies world, also trigger rapid antibody accumulation, when people try to control Microbiome imbalances. For the body to fulfill its maximum potential, the alimentary canal (see Silk Road in Chapter 6), must be relatively problem free and easily maintained with the correct chemistry. If there are problems in your personal Silk Road, you now have the choices to apply a specific chemistry relative to your intentions and belief systems. Finally, once you have upgraded your body and reversed all known and unknown issues at the time, you will continuously have to adjust to your environment, because change is inevitable. In the beginning, Jilly Juice brought about the upgrading process, forcing you to deal with the weaknesses in your body, with the help of modern medicine. Potentially, in the future, you will only be drinking Jilly Juice, minimally, in reaction to a change in your environment, and you will adapt and upgrade faster with minor discomfort and a little mucus. Jilly Juice will help you address the changes in the environment and listen to the indicators and then, you will act accordingly.

Upgrading and Dying are an Individual Journey.

The transference of energy through conversion is the First Law of Thermodynamics, and how you implement this transfer is based upon your knowledge and intentions. Life and death are choices people make directly and indirectly with the knowledge they have at any given time. No matter what, if you are doing the Jilly Juice and upgrading your system, and you are feeling the progress and relaxing, it is an individual journey. When you are lying in bed in hospice, reflecting on your life, regretting some things or nothing at all, is also an individual journey. These are all part of everyone's journey. Regardless, of what is going on in the world and in my household, I will always choose life. I will always and forever continue to drink Jilly Juice and the pure white Salt crystals reflecting the life energy within the ferments and within my well-balanced body. The external environment is always changing, and Jilly Juice will always support my ability to adapt and upgrade to the new environment now, and in the future. If I keep implementing Jilly Juice in my life, I will always be experiencing death and rebirth at the micro level from adaptation, but my potential to keep the macro level intact indefinitely, is almost a sure thing.

BIBLIOGRAPHY

[1] Retrieved: February 15, 2020 https://courses.lumenlearning.com/boundless-chemistry/chapter/the-laws-of-thermodynamics/

[2] Retrieved: February 15, 2020 amnh.org/research/center-for-biodiversity-conservation/about-the-cbc/what-is-biodiversity

[3] Retrieved: February 15, 2020 https://www.livescience.com/53272-what-is-a-virus.html

Cha[4] Retrieved: February 15, 2020 https://www.sciencedirect.com/topics/immunology-and-microbiology/mycovirus

[5] Retrieved: February 15, 2020 https://www.britannica.com/biography/Charles-Darwin

[6] Retrieved: February 15, 2020 https://www.livescience.com/50941-second-law-thermodynamics.html

[7] Retrieved: February 15, 2020 https://www.ncbi.nlm.nih.gov/pmc/articles/PMC4112220/

[8] Retrieved: February 15, 2020 https://www.healthline.com/health/malabsorption

[9] Retrieved: February 18, 2020 https://www.pbs.org/gunsgermssteel/variables/smallpox.html

[11] Retrieved: February 18, 2020 https://www.sciencedirect.com/topics/neuroscience/secretory-immunoglobulin

[12] Retrieved: February 18, 2020 https://www.nbcnews.com/health/womens-health/americans-aren-t-making-enough-babies-replace-ourselves-n956931

[13] Retrieved: February 19, 2020 https://www.sciencedirect.com/topics/agricultural-and-biological-sciences/single-cell-protein

[14] Retrieved: February 19, 2020 https://www.sciencedirect.com/topics/biochemistry-genetics-and-molecular-biology/carbon-source

[15] Retrieved: February 28, 2020 https://www.sciencedaily.com/releases/2013/04/130405064027.htm?fbclid=IwAR0LTrnIE0SToDJWqnsdEFjOovC0GVMQUINxL_QfuSjdi6YSCI-goAC7qVQ

[16] Retrieved: February 19, 2020 https://microbiologyonline.org/index.php/about-microbiology/introducing-microbes/viruses

[17] Retrieved: February 19, 2020 http://www.differencebetween.net/science/health/difference-between-dna-and-rna-viruses/

[18] Retrieved: February 19, 2020 https://ghr.nlm.nih.gov/primer/howgeneswork/protein

[19] Retrieved: February 19, 2020 https://www.ncbi.nlm.nih.gov/books/NBK21523/

[20] Retrieved: February 19, 2020 https://www.nature.com/subjects/viral-evolution

[22] Retrieved: February 21, 2020 http://hosting.astro.cornell.edu/academics/courses/astro201/hydrogen_burn.htm

[23] Retrieved: February 21, 2020 https://courses.lumenlearning.com/boundless-biology/chapter/characteristics-of-fungi/

[24] Retrieved: February 21, 2020 https://ucmp.berkeley.edu/bacteria/bacterialh.html

[25] Retrieved: February 21, 2020 https://www.perdanauniversity.edu.my/killingbacteria/

[26] Retrieved: February 21, 2020 https://depts.washington.edu/ceeh/downloads/FF_Microbiome.pdf

[27] Retrieved: February 21, 2020 https://www.nrcs.usda.gov/wps/portal/nrcs/detailfull/soils/health/biology/?cid=nrcs142p2_053867

[28] Retrieved: February 21, 2020 https://www.cdc.gov/parasites/about.html

[29] Retrieved: February 21, 2020 https://www.caringforkids.cps.ca/handouts/pinworms

[30] Retrieved: February 21, 2020 https://www.ncbi.nlm.nih.gov/pubmed/6370836

[31] Retrieved: February 21, 2020 https://www.ncbi.nlm.nih.gov/pmc/articles/PMC4528493/

[32] Retrieved: February 21, 2020 https://www.sciencedaily.com/releases/2012/11/121107200024.htm

[33] Retrieved: February 21, 2020 https://www.bbc.com/news/health-34857022

[34] Retrieved: February 21, 2020 https://www.sciencedaily.com/releases/2019/04/190411131538.htm

[35] Retrieved: February 21, 2020 https://www.sciencedirect.com/topics/agricultural-and-biological-sciences/agglutination

[36] Retrieved: February 21, 2020 https://www.healthline.com/health/antibody-titer

[37] Retrieved: February 21, 2020 https://www.merriam-webster.com/dictionary/adaptation

[38] Retrieved: February 21, 2020 https://www.hormone.org/your-health-and-hormones/glands-and-hormones-a-to-z/hormones/prostaglandins

[39] Retrieved: February 21, 2020 https://www.ncbi.nlm.nih.gov/pmc/articles/PMC2306303/

[41] Retrieved: February 22, 2020 https://www.tocris.com/pharmacology/sodium-channels

[42] Retrieved: February 22, 2020 https://www.heart.org/en/health-topics/atrial-fibrillation/what-is-atrial-fibrillation-afib-or-af

[43] Retrieved: February 22, 2020 https://www.sciencedirect.com/topics/medicine-and-dentistry/chloride-ion

[44] Retrieved: February 22, 2020 https://www.nhlbi.nih.gov/health-topics/defibrillators

[45] Retrieved: February 22, 2020 https://www.medicalnewstoday.com/articles/319631

[46] Retrieved: February 22, 2020 https://www.ncbi.nlm.nih.gov/pmc/articles/PMC3939772/

[47] Retrieved: February 22, 2020 https://www.ncbi.nlm.nih.gov/pmc/articles/PMC3809489/

[48] Retrieved: February 22, 2020 https://www.ncbi.nlm.nih.gov/pubmed/4055063

[49] Retrieved February 26, 2020 http://www.treasurenet.com/forums/rocks-gems/450473-can-mold-grow-inside-quartz-rocks.html

[50] Retrieved February 26, 2020 https://www.thoughtco.com/quartzite-rock-geology-and-uses-4588608

[51] Retrieved February 26, 2020 https://pennsylvaniawine.com/wp-content/uploads/2017/04/Yeast-Nutrition.pdf

[52] Retrieved February 26, 2020 https://www.medicalnewstoday.com/articles/153188#what-are-electrolytes

[53] Retrieved February 26, 2020 https://www.ncbi.nlm.nih.gov/pmc/articles/PMC1538294/

[54] Retrieved February 26, 2020 https://www.ncbi.nlm.nih.gov/pmc/articles/PMC2117903/

[55] Retrieved February 26, 2020 https://www.med.umich.edu/pfans/pdf/hetm-2016/0416-sugarcancer.pdf

[56] Retrieved February 26, 2020 https://www.britannica.com/science/sugar-chemical-compound

[57] Retrieved February 26, 2020 https://www.ncbi.nlm.nih.gov/pmc/articles/PMC5174149/

[58] Retrieved February 26, 2020 https://www.webmd.com/cholesterol-management/qa/what-are-triglycerides

[59] Retrieved February 26, 2020 https://www.livescience.com/62218-whats-in-a-fat-cell.html

[60] Retrieved February 26, 2020 https://pubchem.ncbi.nlm.nih.gov/compound/Aspartame

[61] Retrieved February 26, 2020 https://www.sciencealert.com/where-body-fat-ends-up-when-you-lose-weight

[62] Retrieved February 26, 2020 https://www.ncbi.nlm.nih.gov/pubmed/15308499

[63] Retrieved February 26, 2020 https://emedicine.medscape.com/article/241094-overview

[64] Retrieved February 26, 2020 https://nurse.plus/become-a-nurse/4-most-commonly-used-iv-fluids/

[65] Retrieved February 26, 2020 https://www.ncbi.nlm.nih.gov/pmc/articles/PMC4053917/

[66] Retrieved February 26, 2020 https://www.mayoclinic.org/diseases-conditions/strep-throat/symptoms-causes/syc-20350338

[67] Retrieved February 26, 2020 https://medlineplus.gov/ency/article/002307.htm

[68] Retrieved February 26, 2020 https://www.ncbi.nlm.nih.gov/pmc/articles/PMC5061687/

[69] Retrieved February 26, 2020 http://learningcentre.usyd.edu.au/wrise/microbiology/overall_structure/os_whole_paper2.html

[70] Retrieved February 26, 2020 https://www.ncbi.nlm.nih.gov/pmc/articles/PMC4328744/

[71] Retrieved February 26, 2020 https://www.ncbi.nlm.nih.gov/pmc/articles/PMC4916494/

[72] Retrieved: February 28, 2020 http://chemistry.elmhurst.edu/vchembook/184ph.html

[73] Retrieved: February 28, 2020 https://www.dictionary.com/browse/pari-mutuel

[74] Retrieved: February 28, 2020 https://www.ncbi.nlm.nih.gov/pmc/articles/PMC4286622/

Retrieved: February 28, 2020 https://www.ncbi.nlm.nih.gov/pubmed/28299478

Retrieved: February 28, 2020 https://www.ncbi.nlm.nih.gov/pmc/articles/PMC5818769/

Retrieved: February 28, 2020 https://www.ncbi.nlm.nih.gov/pmc/articles/PMC2887071/

[75] Retrieved: February 28, 2020 https://www.sciencedirect.com/science/article/abs/pii/S1871141309002674

Retrieved: February 28, 2020 https://www.infoplease.com/encyclopedia/science/biochemistry/concepts/amino-acid

Retrieved: February 28, 2020 https://www.ncbi.nlm.nih.gov/pubmed/18648778

Retrieved: February 28, 2020 https://www.ncbi.nlm.nih.gov/pmc/articles/PMC3671743/

[76] Retrieved: February 28, 2020 https://emedicine.medscape.com/article/241094-overview

[77] Retrieved: February 28, 2020 https://www.britannica.com/topic/Silk-Road-trade-route

[78] Retrieved: February 28, 2020 https://www.advantour.com/silkroad/history-decline.htm

[79] Retrieved: February 28, 2020 https://www.dictionary.com/browse/alimentary-canal

[80] Retrieved: February 28, 2020 https://training.seer.cancer.gov/anatomy/digestive/regions/

[81] Retrieved: February 28, 2020 https://www.livescience.com/37009-human-body.html

[82] Retrieved: February 28, 2020 https://www.ncbi.nlm.nih.gov/pmc/articles/PMC5986486/?fbclid=IwAR12o2tBMIdyt4E2wd8fmU8oJ2h5DmYxSVd9u7V7hyQwjL3dl9t32vNxfuo

[83] Retrieved: March 4, 2020 https://www.nih.gov/news-events/news-releases/structure-viral-harpoon-protein-reveals-how-viruses-enter-cells

Retrieved March 6, 2020 https://www.ncbi.nlm.nih.gov/pmc/articles/PMC5553267/?fbclid=IwAR099dscXjGMewoBaozMXym1_zn1v3PV_ghIH0yQIFhZnUCJnwwVSXsU42c

Retrieved March 6, 2020 https://www.hindawi.com/journals/jpr/2011/610769/?fbclid=IwAR1zJU5uhv81zH7Pk49SnoLOedLk1FeTQK23US04LiNVKNKp4i98ht3pw2A

[84] Retrieved March 4, 2020 https://www.bcm.edu/departments/molecular-virology-and-microbiology/emerging-infections-and-biodefense/mosquitoes?fbclid=IwAR1nybKp09qvwre2zmr56ipfVMmZBXAvzAhOnqK119CdwJIJpIhFXpq2k8E

[85] Retrieved March 4, 2020 https://www.ncbi.nlm.nih.gov/pubmed/12850343

Retrieved March 10, 2020 https://newsroom.ucla.edu/releases/artificial-intelligence-device-detect-moving-parasites-bodily-fluid-earlier-diagnosis

Retrieved March 6, 2020 https://www.ncbi.nlm.nih.gov/books/NBK2265/

Retrieved March 6, 2020 https://www.ncbi.nlm.nih.gov/pubmed/17435136

Retrieved March 6, 2020 https://www.ncbi.nlm.nih.gov/pmc/articles/PMC303053/

Retrieved March 6, 2020 https://www.webmd.com/infertility-and-reproduction/fertility-antisperm-antibodies

Retrieved March 6, 2020 https://www.ncbi.nlm.nih.gov/pubmed/2237758

Retrieved March 6, 2020 https://medlineplus.gov/ency/article/003592.htm

Retrieved March 6, 2020 https://www.ncbi.nlm.nih.gov/pmc/articles/PMC4716500/

Retrieved March 6, 2020 https://www.ncbi.nlm.nih.gov/pubmed/3283249

[86] Retrieved March 6, 2020 https://www.britannica.com/science/mucus

Retrieved March 6, 2020 https://medlineplus.gov/blood.html

[87] Retrieved March 6, 2020 https://www.medicalnewstoday.com/articles/326020

Retrieved March 6, 2020 https://www.webmd.com/vitamins/ai/ingredientmono-538/kombucha

Retrieved March 6, 2020 https://www.ncbi.nlm.nih.gov/pmc/articles/PMC4188582/

Retrieved March 6, 2020 https://www.medicalnewstoday.com/articles/320911

Retrieved March 6, 2020 https://www.ncbi.nlm.nih.gov/pmc/articles/PMC4022204/

Retrieved March 6, 2020 https://www.ncbi.nlm.nih.gov/pmc/articles/PMC3609166/

Retrieved March 6, 2020 https://www.ncbi.nlm.nih.gov/pmc/articles/PMC6308289/

https://www.ncbi.nlm.nih.gov/pmc/articles/PMC5788933/

[88] Retrieved March 6, 2020 http://chemocare.com/chemotherapy/what-is-chemotherapy/the-immune-system.aspx

[89] Retrieved March 6, 2020 https://www.psychologytoday.com/us/blog/not-born-yesterday/201210/are-you-left-or-right-brain-dominant

[90] Retrieved March 6, 2020 https://www.who.int/health-topics/coronavirus

[91] Retrieved March 6, 2020 https://www.healthline.com/health/autophagy

[92 Retrieved March 8, 2020 https://www.cancercenter.com/what-is-cancer

[93] Retrieved March 9, 2020 https://www.ncbi.nlm.nih.gov/pmc/articles/PMC6240559/

[94] Retrieved March 10, 2020 https://www.uspharmacist.com/article/addressing-hypoglycemic-emergencies

[95] Retrieved March 18, 2020 https://www.innerbody.com/anatomy/respiratory

[96] Retrieved May 2, 2020 https://www.healthline.com/health/adh